PALMER MILLS

The History of a Stockport Cotton Spinning Mill

Fig.1 Frontispiece. Aerial view of Palmer No.2 Mill from the north-west. The engine house of Vernon No.1 Mill can be seen to the left and top left, across the river, is New Bridge Lane Mill. (10/05/1989)

PALMER MILLS

The History of a Stockport Cotton Spinning Mill

Roger N. Holden

Stockport

2017

Roger N.Holden, 35 Victoria Road, Stockport, Cheshire, SK1 4AT, UK.

A CIP record for this book is available from the British Library.

ISBN 978-0-9956977-1-3

Created in MS Word 2010 and typeset in Times New Roman by Roger N.Holden.

Produced by www.lulu.com. Printed on demand.

CONTENTS

West Riding of Yorkshire
Lancashire
Cheshire
Derbyshire
Skipton
Barnoldswick
Earby
Clitheroe
Colne
Nelson
Kirkham
Great Harwood
Padiham
Burnley
Preston
Accrington
Blackburn
Rawtenstall
Todmorden
Haslingden
Darwen
Bacup
Eccleston
Chorley
Ramsbottom
Littleborough
WEAVING DISTRICT
Rochdale
Bury
Heywood
SPINNING DISTRICT
Bolton
Radcliffe
Middleton
Wigan
Farnworth
Oldham
SD
SE
Mossley
Leigh
Salford
Ashton-under-Lyne
Stalybridge
Golborne
Manchester
Dukinfield
Glossop
Hyde
STOCKPORT
Warrington
New Mills
River Mersey
Bollington
SJ
SK
N
Weaving towns
Spinning towns
0
10Km
THE LOCATION OF STOCKPORT WITHIN
THE LANCASHIRE COTTON DISTRICT

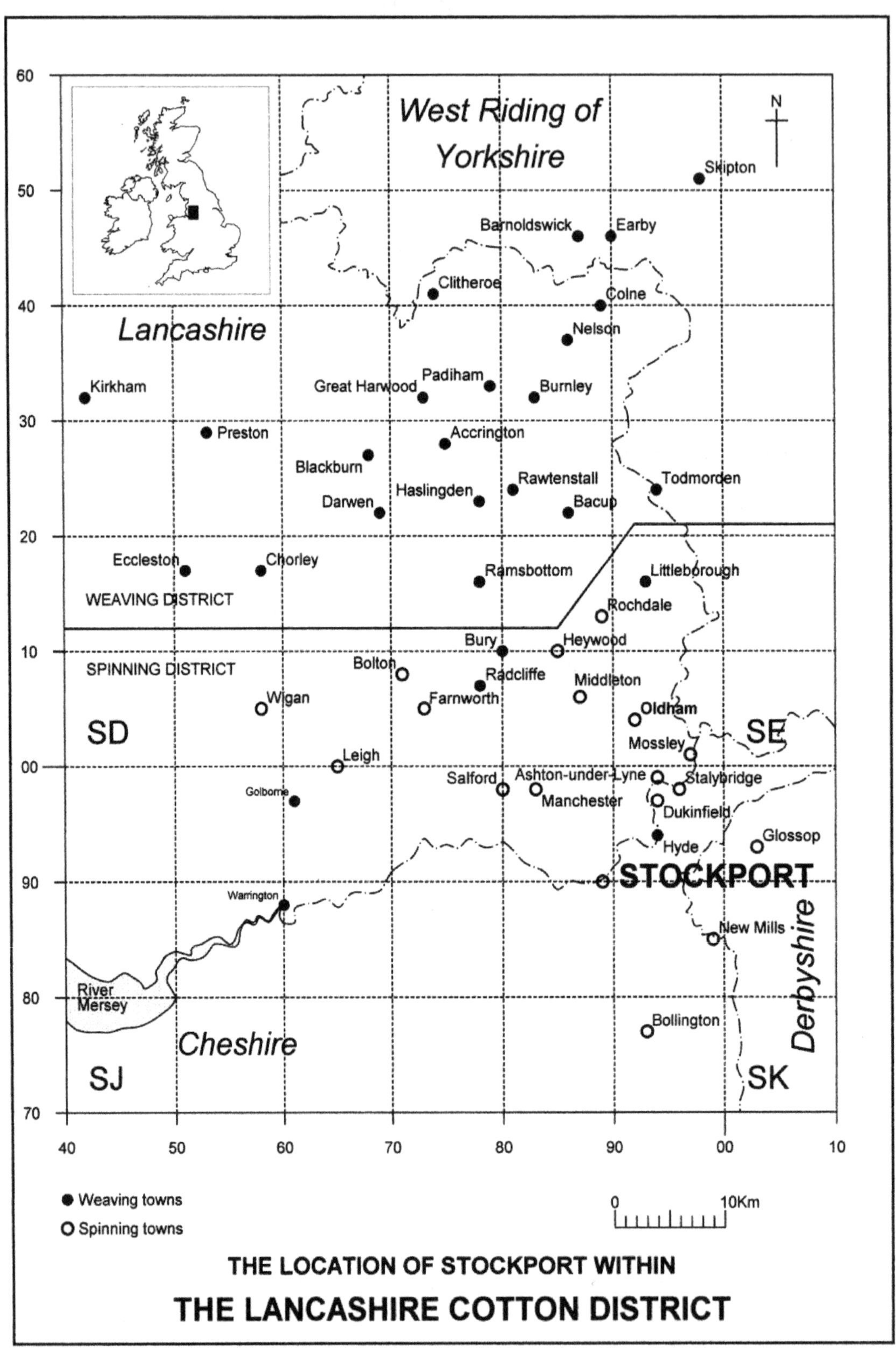

Fig.2

PREFACE

This essay was originally written in 2001, after Palmer Mills had been demolished. Copies were deposited at relevant places, particularly the Stockport Local Studies Library, but there was no prospect at that time in publishing it to make it more generally available. Such a study would not command sufficient sales for publication in its own right and as it stood it would have been too long for a journal article, while hardly containing the generality of scope required for the more academic journals. However, digitisation has changed that and made self-publication on-line possible. As copies are only printed to order, it is feasible to do this even if only a few copies, far fewer than for a conventional print run, are likely to be sold. Conversely, it does not matter if demand is greater than originally estimated.

Some revision of the text has been made for publication and more illustrations have been included, another benefit of digitisation. A number of errors have been corrected in both text and illustrations. Palmer Mills were demolished before the era of digital photography so, apart from the recent views of the site, all photographs are from black and white prints or colour slides. Not all are of the highest quality, some of the colour slides have suffered in the digitisation process, but are included here for their historic value. While the author had been unable to gain access to the surviving No.2 Mill before demolition in 1999 he was able to closely observe and photograph the demolition process.

A similar essay on Chadderton Mill, an Oldham cotton spinning mill, has also been made available in the same way.

ENGINEERING UNITS

Current archaeological building survey practice is to survey everything in metric units, but this approach seems fundamentally wrong for buildings designed and built to imperial units to house equipment constructed to imperial units. If metric units are used these buildings become difficult to understand and significant dimensions are obscured by becoming 'funny numbers'. Therefore in this study imperial units are used, with metric equivalents being given where appropriate.

ACKNOWLEDGEMENTS

Norman Redhead, Deputy County Archaeologist, granted access to the Textile Mill Survey archive, including aerial photographs, which was then held as part of the County Sites and Monuments Record, Greater Manchester Archaeology Unit, University of Manchester.

John Rose Associates, at the request of Norman Redhead, provided a copy of their Archaeological Survey Report on Palmer Mill.

The staffs of Stockport Local Heritage Library, Oldham Local Studies Library, the Lancashire Archives and the National Archives.

Note that fig.25 is taken from a copy held by the Stockport Heritage Trust. It was thought that this photograph comes from the collections of the Stockport Local Heritage Library but no copy can be traced in their collections. Fig.26 is from a photograph by N.S.Roberts of Rochdale, a pioneer of aerial photography, but it has not been possible to trace a copy of the original. The image here is taken from a photocopy, hence its poor quality. This photocopy was in the possession of Stockport Local Heritage Library in 2001, but cannot now be traced. These two pictures are important because they are the only know views showing the complete Palmer Mills complex from the north.

All photographs and drawings are by the author unless otherwise stated.

STOCKPORT, 1907

SHOWING THE LOCATION OF PALMER MILLS

Based on 1:10 560 Ordnance Survey of Cheshire, 1911 edition, surveyed 1907, sheets 10SE & 19NE. Not to scale

Fig.3

1. INTRODUCTION

This is a detailed study of one particular cotton spinning mill but seeks also to put it into the wider contexts of the cotton industry in Stockport and Lancashire. Although located in Cheshire, being south of the River Mersey, Stockport formed part of the Lancashire cotton region (fig.2). The Lancashire cotton industry as it developed from the late eighteenth century onwards was located in the south-east part of the county centred on Manchester, spilling over the border into Cheshire, Derbyshire and the West Riding of Yorkshire. In the early years of the industry Manchester itself was an important production centre, but as the nineteenth century progressed it became increasingly the merchant centre, production being carried out elsewhere. Production of cloth from raw cotton requires first the spinning of yarn and then the weaving of yarn into cloth. The differing physical and managerial requirements of these two processes led to specialisation between spinning and weaving mills and firms. This specialisation also became geographical with weaving concentrated in the area known as East Lancashire centred on Blackburn and Burnley. On the other hand, spinning predominated in the ring of towns surrounding Manchester including Stockport, Ashton-under-Lyne, Oldham, Rochdale and Bolton.

In the early nineteenth century, Stockport in Cheshire was second only to Manchester as centre of cotton production.[1] In 1811 there were 3 440 000 spinning spindles in Lancashire, of which 466 000, or 13·4%, were in Stockport compared with Manchester's 1 103 000, 32·1% of the total. But after the 1830s the town fell behind and from the 1860s onwards could not compete with the large mills being constructed in Oldham and Bolton (fig.5). The old mills of Stockport were too small to house very long mules then being installed and some survived by moving to doubling, that is the process of twisting together two or more spun yarns to produce thread, and Stockport became a centre for this trade. However, in the 1880s there was some revival of spinning with new mills being constructed comparable in size with those in Oldham. The first of these was Vernon Mill of 1881, followed by Palmer, the subject of this study. After the completion of Stockport Ring Mill in 1891, the industry stagnated and the number of spindles in Stockport fell slightly during the 1890s. But the Edwardian period was a boom period with many large mills being built in Lancashire. The Stockport area participated in this with several new mills being built including the Stockport Ring 2 & 3 Mills, Broadstone Mills at Reddish, Goyt Mill at Marple, Ark Ring Mill at Bredbury and Pear Mill at Bredbury. In 1911 there were 58 million spindles in Lancashire of which 2·57 million, 4·4%, were in Stockport. This compares with 16·4 million, 28%, in Oldham. The number of spindles in Stockport further increased after 1911 to reach a maximum of 2·85 million in 1920. These figures include spinning and doubling spindles; in 1912, the first year for which separate figures are available, 9·9% of spindles in Stockport were for doubling. This proportion increased in the following years and in 1920 12% were doubling.[2]

The years immediately after the First World War were boom years for the Lancashire cotton industry but this boom had collapsed by 1921. In retrospect this marked the beginning of the end for the industry. There was a slight recovery in the mid-1920s but thereafter the path was downward and the industry in Stockport followed this decline. From the late 1920s onwards mills began to close never to be re-opened. Decline took the next half century, with spinning ceasing in Stockport with the closure of Greg's Albert Mills at Reddish in 1982.

Palmer Mills were located in the Portwood area, to the east of Stockport town centre, alongside the River Goyt (fig.3 & 4). The Portwood area, originally in the Township of Brinnington, bounded on the north by the River Tame and the south by the River Goyt, had been an early site for the location of cotton mills.[3] These rivers provided ample water supplies for early water powered mills, a complex of weirs and tunnels being constructed to tap this resource, and later for supplying the engines of steam powered mills.

---

1 Mike Williams with D.A.Farnie, *Cotton Mills in Greater Manchester* (Preston: Carnegie, 1992), 24-6.

2 1811 figures from Crompton's Census. 1911 and later figures from John Worrall's *Cotton Spinners & Manufacturers Directory for Lancashire*. Stockport here means the Stockport District as defined by Worrall which included the Borough of Stockport, Birch Vale, Cheadle, Compstall, Furness Vale, Hayfield, Hazel Grove, Heaton Mersey, Heaton Norris, Marple, Mellor, New Mills, Reddish, Romiley, Strines, Whaley Bridge, Woodley and Bredbury. This is basically the same area as the current Metropolitan Borough of Stockport, plus the southern part of the High Peak district of Derbyshire.

3 Note that the River Mersey is now considered to start from the confluence of the River Goyt and the River Tame. However, on maps up to and including the 1851 Ordnance Survey the River Mersey was regarded as starting upstream of this point. This explains why the street to the north of Palmer Mills is

Palmer Mills ceased spinning in the 1930s and were partially demolished, leaving just the No.2 Mill, which survived until 1999. Thus it was still standing at the time of the Greater Manchester Textile Mills Survey, conducted in the mid-1980s by the Greater Manchester Archaeological Unit in conjunction with the Royal Commission on the Historical Monuments of England. The results of this survey were published in the book *Cotton Mills in Greater Manchester* in 1992.[4] Only a level C survey of Palmer Mill was carried out consisting of brief external survey with terrestrial and aerial photographs.[5] Before demolition of the mill, at the request of the Greater Manchester County Archaeologist, a survey of the mill was carried out for the developers by John Rose Associates, Chartered Planning & Development Consultants, of Poynton. This survey is of value for the site plans included and the photographic record of the interior.

The current study, therefore, arose from a desire to provide a more detailed account of the mill and is developed from notes made during the author's earlier research into the works of Stott & Sons, the Oldham mill architects.[6] Additional documentary sources, listed at the end of this study, have been investigated. These are principally the company files held by the National Archives, Kew, and the relevant machinery orders contained in the Platt-Saco-Lowell Archive at the Lancashire Archives, Preston.

known as Mersey Street.

4 Williams with Farnie, *Cotton Mills in Greater Manchester*.

5 National Monuments Record No.53373, Greater Manchester Sites and Monuments Record No.2529.

6 Roger N.Holden, *Stott & Sons: Architects of the Lancashire Cotton Mill* (Lancaster: Carnegie, 1998).

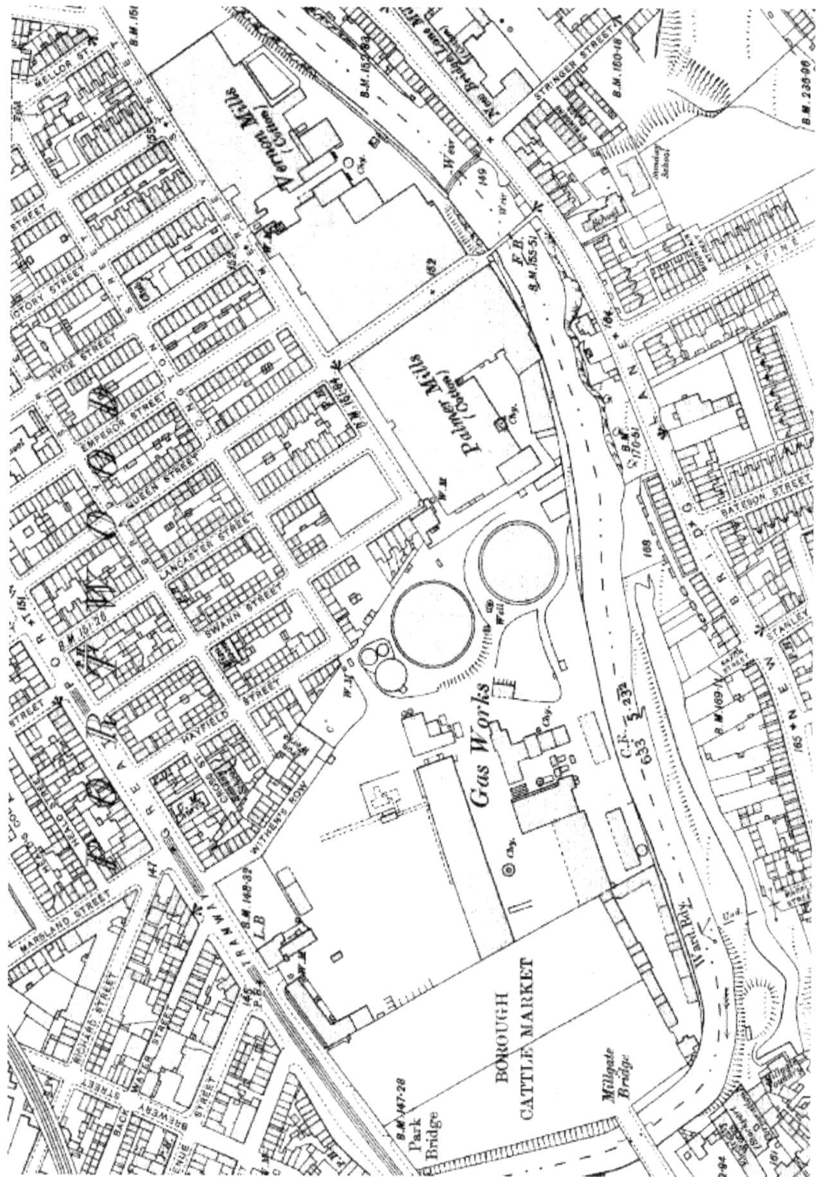

Fig.4 Extract from Ordnance Survey 1:2500 sheet Cheshire 10.15, 1910 edition, revised to 1907. This shows Palmer Mills and the adjacent Vernon Mills at their fullest extent. The footbridge marked over the river between Queen Street and New Bridge Lane was known as Captain's Bridge.

Reproduction not to scale.

Installed Spindles in the Lancashire Cotton Industry
and in Stockport
1800-1959
Lancashire
Stockport
Palmer Mills built
Palmer No.1 Mill built
Palmer No.2 Mill built
Palmer Mills closed
Millions of Spindles
0
10
20
30
40
50
60
1790
1800
1810
1820
1830
1840
1850
1860
1870
1880
1890
1900
1910
1920
1930
1940
1950
1960
From estimates for spindles in Great Britain, Farnie (2004), 23. Figures reduced by 6% to approximate for Lancashire.
Worrall's Lancashire Textile Directory, 1882-1959.
Interpolated between 1811, Samuel Crompton's Census of the Cotton Industry, and 1887, no other data in this region.

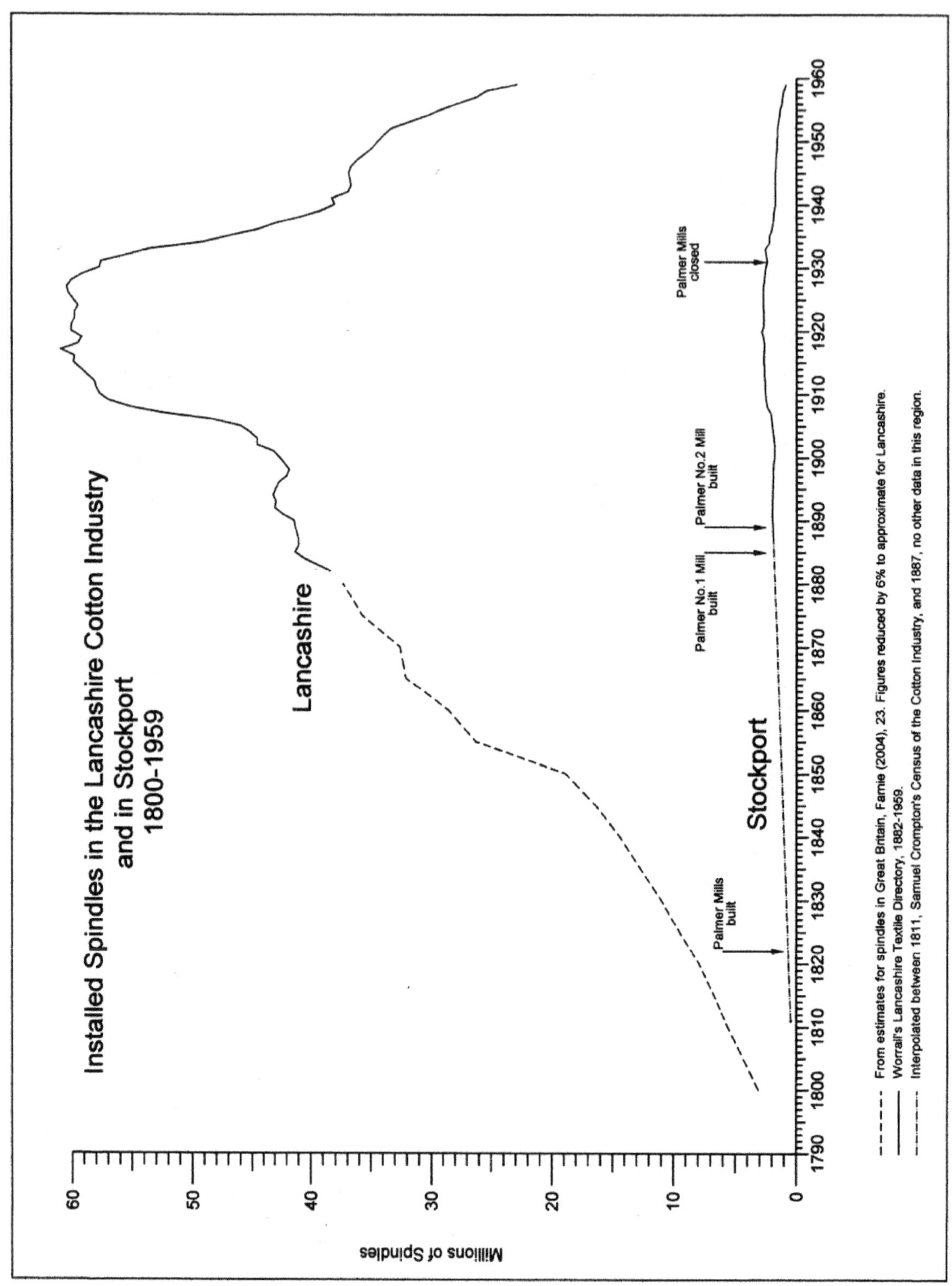

Fig.5

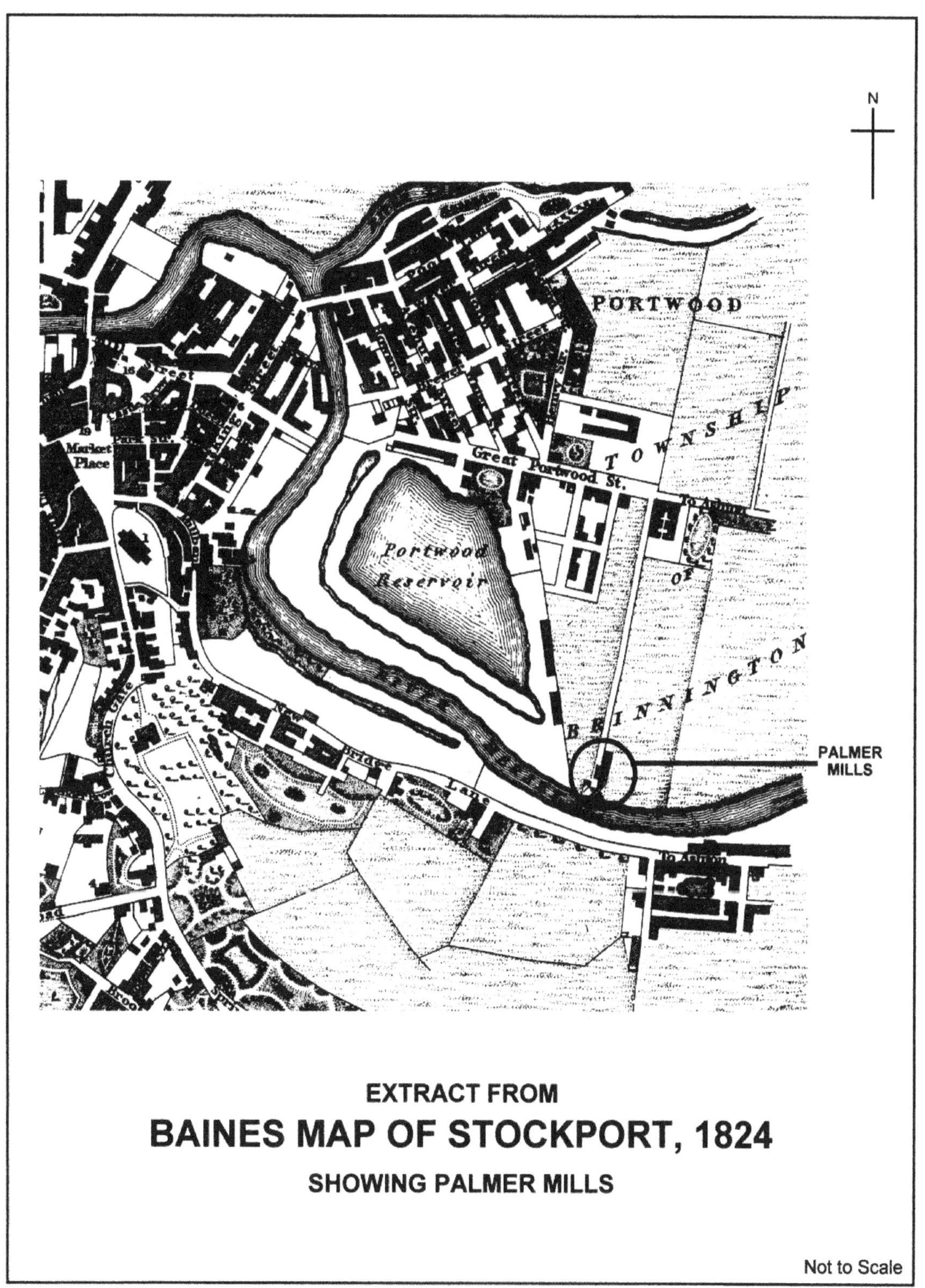

EXTRACT FROM

BAINES MAP OF STOCKPORT, 1824

SHOWING PALMER MILLS

Fig.6

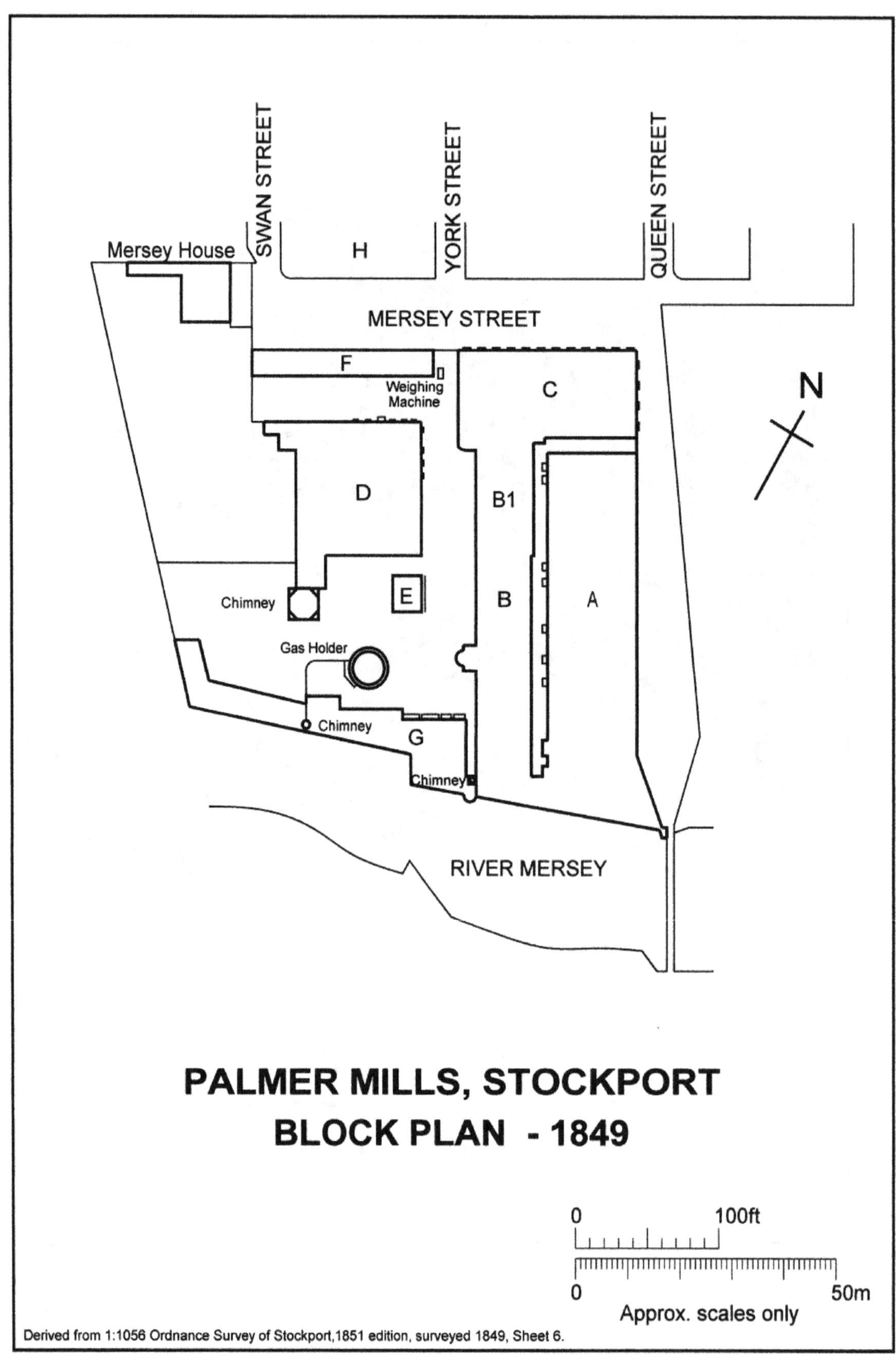

Fig.7
Note: the letters are referred to in the description given in the text.

2. THE ORIGINAL MILL

The origins of Palmer Mills can be traced back to the first quarter of the nineteenth century and are reputed by later sources to have been established in 1822 by James Marshall.[7] They may thus have been one of the eight mills reported by the *Stockport Advertiser* to be under construction during August of that year.[8] However, James Marshall was established as a cotton spinner before 1822 and Crompton's census lists him as operating 504 jenny spindles in Stockport.[9] Jennies were unpowered, hand-operated, machines and these could have been located in a workshop somewhere in town, not necessarily on the Palmer Mills site. He does not appear in the 1814-15 edition of *The Commercial Directory*, but the 1816-17 edition lists him as a cotton spinner in Portwood, but unfortunately does not give the name of the mill. That he was a well established cotton spinner is confirmed by a report in the *Stockport Advertiser* of 13 September 1822 that on the previous day eight men, described as journeymen cotton spinners, had been committed by the Stockport Petty Sessions to the House of Correction at Knutsford for two months for combination and quitting the employment of Mr.Marshall of Portwood.[10] Again, no mill name is given.

The subsequent progress of James Marshall can be traced from directory entries. In *Baines's Lancashire* of 1824 he appears as a cotton spinner and warp maker, although his address is again simply given as Portwood.[11] By the time of *Pigot's Commercial Directory* for 1828-9 he had also started weaving as well as spinning, being listed as a cotton spinner and manufacturer. Again his address is simply given as Portwood although the title of the firm is given as James Marshall & Sons showing that his sons had now joined the business. The name Palmer Mills first appears in *The Stockport Directory* for 1837. No reason can be given as to why the mills were named Palmer which sounds like a personal name. Later reports state that he let out Palmer Mill to 'small masters', presumably on a 'room-and-turning' basis, but the directory entries make clear that he also operated there himself.[12]

The map of Stockport published in *Baines's Lancashire* (fig.6), dated 1824, does indeed show a building on the site but unfortunately does not actually name this or any other of the mills in the town. However, it can be seen to be comparable in size with other known mill buildings in Stockport, such as those in Hopes Carr, and can be assumed to be the first building on the Palmer Mills site while the unnamed road leading down to it is what later was named York Street and more recently Lancaster Street.[13] The accuracy of this survey is not known, but scaling off it suggests that the main, long rectangular plan, building to the east of the site had dimensions of around 170 feet (51·8m) long by 35 feet (10·7m) deep, although the 1851 Ordnance Survey would suggest a depth of 40 feet. Two extensions are shown to the west of this building. This building is believed to have been six storeys in height, this may include a basement. For comparison, the *Stockport Advertiser* reported in November 1822 on a mill under construction for Johnson and Scott which was 87 feet (26·5m) long by 39 feet (11·9m) deep and six stories high.[14] The type of construction of this first mill, whether fireproof or not, is not known. There are suggestions that the first fireproof mills in Stockport were constructed during the 1820s but other mills of contemporary date in Hopes Carr were non-fireproof, consisting of timber beams supported by cast iron columns while the earliest identified fireproof mills in Stockport, at Wear Mill and at Wellington Mill, date

---

7 'The Mayors of Stockport No.XII James Marshall', *Cheshire County News,* 27/3/1896 (note this is his son also named James).

8 Unheaded paragraph, *Stockport Advertiser*, 16/8/1822, 4c.

9 'Statistics obtained in 1811 by Samuel Crompton showing the number of spindles on the Mule, Jenny & Throstle and the factories employing these machines', Bolton Archives and Local Studies, GB125.677. G.W.Daniels, 'Samuel Crompton's Census of the Cotton Industry in 1811', *Economic History* II (1930-3), 107-10.

10 *Stockport Advertiser*, 16/8/1822, 4c.

11 Edward Baines, *History, Directory and Gazetteer of the County Palatine of Lancaster* (1824), Vol.2, 719-32. Stockport in Cheshire appears as an appendix to this work because of its close connection with Lancashire.

12 Room-and-turning because the mill owner provide the 'room' in which small masters could install their own machinery and the power, 'turning', to drive them from a steam engine. This system died out in the spinning industry after 1850 but persisted in the weaving industry, where it was known as 'room-and-power'.

13 This renaming took place at some time between the sale of the mill in 1884 and the Ordnance Survey of 1895. During the same period Swan Street acquired another 'n' to become Swann Street (fig. 4).

14 *Stockport Advertiser*, 15/11/1822, 4c.

from around 1828 to 1830.[15] The map tells us nothing about power supply but, although located on the river, it shows no water courses to the Palmer Mills site suggesting that it was steam powered. A ready supply of water was vital for operating a steam engine, for both boiler feed water and condensing water. The river provided a ready supply, without which a reservoir, or lodge, would have been needed.[16] The extensions to the west side could suggest a boiler house. At this date a steam engine would have been a beam engine and such were normally installed internal to the mill rather than in a projecting engine house as in later mills. *Baines's Lancashire* states that in 1824 that there were in Stockport, including the townships of Heaton Norris and Portwood, 47 cotton factories worked by 62 steam engines and water wheels of aggregate power of 1880hp (1·4MW), that is an average of 30hp (22·4kW).[17] There is no information as to the number or type of spindles installed in the mill. Crompton's census of 1811 gives a total of 459 856 spindles in the town, of which 352 396 were mule spindles, 83 712 were jenny spindles and the remaining 23 748 were throstle spindles. Stockport at that date had a disproportionately large number of jenny spindles compared with other districts. We do not know how the situation had changed over the decade following this census. On the assumption that Palmer Mill was powered, it is suggested that James Marshall built Palmer Mills in order to move from jenny spinning to throstles or, most likely, mules. For cotton spinning, mules were replacing jennies and throstles, although throstles continued to be used for particular types of yarn. These mules would have been the semi-powered mules which, after the introduction of the self-acting mule, came to be referred to as 'hand' mules. On these machines the spinning part of the cycle was carried out by power while the winding part was performed by hand. *The Stockport Directory* of 1837 clearly describes James Marshall & Sons as being cotton spinners and manufacturers by power.

In 1837 the private address of James Marshall is given as Whitebank House while his two sons, James, junior, and John lived at Brinnington Mount and Mersey House respectively.[18] Mersey House had been built some time after 1824 and adjoined the mill, suggesting that John was the partner acting as manager of the mill. James Marshall, junior, was Mayor of Stockport in 1848. The Marshall business was later extended. In 1842 they were occupying Park Bridge Mill, which stood on the triangle of land between Raffald Street (later Corporation Street), Warren Street and the river.[19] This later became Faulder's Cocoa Works (fig.75 & 76). By 1851 they also had a mill in Heaton Norris and offices at New Cannon Street in Manchester. By 1860 they were no longer at Park Bridge Mill but by 1864 they were also at Waterside Mills, Disley. In 1872, however, they are listed only as cotton spinners and are no longer at Waterside Mill. When the firm ceased to exist is unclear but Palmer Mills were put up for auction in February 1884. No doubt the firm had suffered the fate of many private partnerships, the partners having died without anybody to take over.

The 1851 edition of the 1:1056 Ordnance Survey map, which was surveyed in 1849, shows that Palmer Mills had been considerably extended since 1824 (fig.7) and comparison with later maps shows that the old mills had reached their maximum extent by this date. Lack of intermediate maps means that we cannot give any dates for these buildings, but the notice for the auction of the mills in 1884 states that there were three separate Chief Rents on the site suggesting an expansion in two stages after construction of the initial mill. The mills occupied a site bounded to the south by the river, still marked as the River Mersey, the Portwood Reservoir of the Stockport Water Works to the west, Mersey Street to the north and Queen Street to the east. The area to the north of the mill, between it and Great Portwood Street had developed considerably since Baines map of 1824. In addition to considerable housing development there was now a wooden footbridge over the river immediately to the east of the mill; this became known as Captain's Bridge. The large house adjoining the mill, Mersey House, was evidently the residence of the manager. The

---

15 Peter Arrowsmith, *Stockport: A History* (Stockport: Stockport Metropolitan Borough Council, 1997), 146. Williams with Farnie, *Cotton Mills in Greater Manchester*, 179-180. Peter Arrowsmith, 'Wellington Mill, Daw Bank, Stockport' in *Recording Stockport's Past* (Stockport: Stockport Metropolitan Borough Council, 1996), 44-51.

16 Roger N.Holden, 'Water Supplies for Steam-powered Textile Mills', *Industrial Archaeology Review*, 21:1 (1999), 41-51.

17 Baines's wording is slightly ambiguous as to whether the 62 is just steam engines or water wheels as well.

18 Brinnington Mount is shown at the north-east corner of fig.3, Whitebank House being just off the map.

19 *Plans of all the Mills & c. in the Township of Stockport relative to their assessment to the Poor Rate* (1842), folio 13. Note that this volume does not include Palmer Mills because Portwood was in the Township of Brinnington.

presence of a large chimney shows that by 1849 the mill was dependent on steam power and the river would have provided a source of water for this purpose.

The 1849 Ordnance Survey shows two parallel long, narrow, buildings, A and B, at right angles to the river with a rectangular building, C, immediately to the north and joined to the building B. These would have been multi-storey mills, used for spinning and possibly also for weaving. Before 1850 it was not uncommon for power looms to be installed in multi-storey mills, on the ground floor and sometimes on upper floors as well. While demolition of the old buildings was in progress in 1889, part collapsed with fatal consequences and the reports in the *Stockport Advertiser* state that the part which collapsed and the adjoining buildings were of six storeys. The part which collapsed was described as having been constructed as an infill of 42 feet (12·8m) wide and 74 feet (22·6m) long between two existing buildings.[20] Building B appears to incorporate the building shown on Baines' 1824 map while the northern end, labelled B1, increases slightly in width. Scaling off the map gives the dimensions of the southern, narrower section to be about 170 feet (51·8m) long by 40 feet (12·2m) deep which is in agreement with the dimensions scaled off the Baines map and so must form the original building. The northern section, B1, scales to about 70 feet (21·3m) long and must be the later in-fill building. The projection on the west wall of building B is probably a staircase tower, although Baines shows a much larger projection here. Building A is wider at around 60 feet (18·3m). Building C, attached to building B, was retained when the new mills were built and was five storeys plus an attic in height (fig.15) and around 120 feet (36·6m) in length by 55 feet (16·8m) deep.

Building D is about 85 feet (25·9m) square and may have been a single storey weaving shed. Block E looks as if it could be a boiler house, but it is known that later the boiler house occupied block G adjoining the river. At this date G clearly incorporated a gas works, indicated by the presence of the gas holder. The two chimneys shown here would appear to be associated with the gas works, the main chimney, retained when the new mills were built, being that attached to building D. The 1884 auction notice refers to a '...mechanics shop, stables and other buildings'. Some of these may have been located in the long narrow building F, fronting Mersey Street adjoining the main entrance and weighbridge. There are no obvious engine houses, but at this date they would have been beam engine houses, internal to the mill driving via gearing and a main vertical drive shaft. The later portion of B was a fireproof building with concrete floors laid on brick arches which sprang from iron girders supported by iron columns. There were eight bays of 9 feet centre to centre the brick arches running transversely across the mill so that the thrust of the arches of the end bays was taken by the walls of the existing buildings, the in-fill simply consisting of the two side walls with no end walls of its own. This led to a collapse while being demolished because the southern part of building B was demolished first and once this was gone there was nothing to support the outward thrust of the arches. Building C was also of fire proof construction, with single brick arches spanning between cast-iron beams supported by cast-iron columns (fig.8 & 9).

The 1872 edition of the 1:1250 Ordnance Survey shows the basic outline of the mill unchanged from 1849 but the gas holder has disappeared and there have been changes to the buildings, G, fronting the river. No doubt gas supply was now being taken from the Stockport Gas Works, which had been constructed on the adjacent site previously occupied by the reservoir of the water works, and this building then became the boiler house. This map also shows a building marked 'Store' in the area bounded by Swan Street, Mersey Street and York Street, marked H (fig.7), which had been constructed since the 1849 map. This is mentioned in the 1884 auction notice as being a warehouse. The auction notice also includes a plot of land facing Swan Street, which must have been the plot immediately to the north of Mersey House, shown vacant on the 1872 Ordnance Survey. A further plot of land included in the auction was that facing Mersey Street and bounded by York Street and Queen Street, also shown as vacant in 1872.

Exactly when Palmer Mills ceased to operate is not known but they were put up for auction at the White Lion Hotel, Stockport, on Friday, 15 February 1884, at seven o'clock in the evening. Advertisements for the auction appeared in the *Stockport Advertiser* for the previous three weeks.[21] This notice states that the sale was pursuant to a judgement of the High Court of Justice, Chancery Division, in an action Alcock v.Banner of 1881, suggesting that the mills may have ceased operating some years previously. The mills were offered for sale in four lots; lot one covered the mills themselves together with Mersey House; lot 2 was the building plot facing Swan Street; lot 3 was the site between Swan Street and York Street containing

---

20 'The Palmer Mills Disaster', *Stockport Advertiser,* 22/3/1889, 4e. 'The Palmer Mills Disaster - The Adjourned Inquest', *Stockport Advertiser,* 29/3/1889, 7g.

21 Notice of auction, *Stockport Advertiser*, 1, 8 & 15/2/1884, 4d.

the warehouse and lot 4 was the building plot between York Street and Queen Street. The property was initially to be offered in one lot and if not sold as four separate lots. In the event the auction failed to sell the mills and they were put up for sale by private treaty.

The auction notice does not suggest whether or not it was intended to try and sell the mills as a going concern. They may have been out of operation for some years and would have been too old and obsolete to make them viable as a going concern. During the previous two decades Stockport had begun to decline as a cotton centre under competition from the new mills being built in Oldham and elsewhere. During the 1870s there was a lot of mill building in Oldham by the new limited liability companies, the 'Oldham Limiteds', who built mills of much greater size and, in particular, greater width to house longer mules. These mills were typically of 130 feet (39·6m) in width housing mules of 1000 spindles and more. The mills in Stockport dating from the early part of the century were much smaller, only 40 to 50 feet in width, and could not compete. Some mills were turned over to other uses, for example Wellington Mill which was taken over by Ward Brothers as a hat works in the late 1890s. Other old mills survived within the textile industry by specialising, in particular into doubling and candlewick yarn spinning. Doubled yarn was produced by twisting two or more single yarns together and was used for a variety of purposes. Candlewick was produced by spinning cotton waste on the condenser system, producing a yarn whose structure was more akin to woollen yarns. Shaw Heath Mill was turned over to the spinning of worsted yarns in around 1890; although only built about 30 years previously its size made it obsolete as a cotton mill. The other approach was 'if you cannot beat them, join them' and construct new mills run by limited liability companies.

The Oldham limited liability mill building boom was at its height in the mid-1870s. Although there had been some earlier attempts to form limited liability cotton companies in Stockport none of these were successful and it was not until 1881 that the first successful company was formed. This was the Vernon Cotton Spinning Company Limited formed to build a mill on a site just upstream from Palmer Mills. There may have been some Oldham influence in the formation of this company as Joseph Stott of Oldham was appointed architect. Both Joseph and his wife Sarah were shareholders in the company. Building work was under way by autumn and a foundation stone laying ceremony was performed on Monday 28 October 1881.[22] Mr.Twyford, the Chairman of the Board of Directors, claimed they would have an advantage over Oldham in that the mill would cost 4s or 5s less per spindle than the cheapest mill in Oldham. They built a second mill in 1884.

[22] 'Jottings and Useful Hints', *Textile Manufacturer*, 15/11/1881, 424.

Fig.8 Interior of block C of the Old Mill, which was retained as part of the new mill, showing the single brick-arch construction and new hopper bale openers installed in 1915.
'Interesting Installation of Opening Machinery', *Textile Recorder*, (33: 389), 15/8/1915, 102 (fig.2).

Fig.9 Interior of block C of the Old Mill, which was retained as part of the new mill, showing the single brick-arch construction and new hopper feeders and mixing stacks installed in 1915.
'Interesting Installation of Opening Machinery', *Textile Recorder*, (33: 389), 15/8/1915, 102 (fig.3).

Fig.10 Vernon No.1 Mill of 1881. Photographed from in front of Palmer No.2 Mill, Vernon No.2 Mill of 1884 occupied the area between the two mills. The water tower and far end of the mill were added in c.1900 and was then rebuilt after a fire in 1902. (12/01/1992)

Fig.11 Rear view of Vernon No.1 Mill. Engine and boiler house nearest the camera. The engine house was not damaged in the 1902 fire so is as originally built in 1881. Horns motor showrooms on the left occupies the site of the No.2 Mill. (12/01/1992)

3. FORMATION OF THE COMPANY TO BUILD A NEW MILL

The ultimate fate of the Palmer Mills was purchase by a newly formed company with the express intention of demolishing parts and constructing a new mill on the site. Councillor John Burtinshaw was unable to attend the auction but when he heard of its failure he became concerned that the mill would be pulled down and replaced by houses or shops. He communicated with Thomas Alcock and found that the reserve bid was £4500 and offered to take it at that price. There were some opposing parties to the purchase and it was not until Friday, 23 May 1884 that the contract was confirmed conditional upon 10% of the purchase money being paid. He considered that a limited liability company should be formed to work the mill and he called a meeting of interested persons on the evening of the following Tuesday, 27 May, to form a provisional directorate. This was a small, private, meeting with only 15 persons present who were: Alderman Johnson, Councillor Burtinshaw, F.Hornbuckle, William Ward, J. W. Swain, Jonathon Noden, William Bell, S.Kershaw, W.Helm, William White, Benjamin Tideswell, W. Charlesworth, W. Linney, Burtinshaw jnr.[*sic*] and S.Hope. This was in fact the day after a meeting to consider the formation of a company to build a mill in Heaton Norris; Councillor Burtinshaw had also attended this meeting but the project came to nothing. One speaker at this meeting, Warren Blackshaw, claimed that a number of attempts to float companies in Stockport had failed because they were using old buildings.[23]

The name Palmer Mills Company Limited was adopted as they might wish to carry out weaving as well as spinning. The alternative title of Stockport Mill Company was considered but rejected because this name had previously been used by a company which had failed. The exact form of the new mill had not been decided at this stage. In particular it was to be left to the directors whether to continue mule spinning or adopt the newer system of ring spinning. However, it was thought that while they would build a new mill, not all of the present structure would be demolished. Some of the existing buildings could be retained, including the chimney and managers house, both of which were considered to be worth £1500. The new mill, they hoped, would cost 15s per spindle. The Manchester and County Bank were to be bankers, Mr.Charlesworth secretary *pro tem* and William Smith solicitor, but no mention is made of architects at this stage.

Eleven people were to form the provisional directorate, including four persons who were not present at the meeting. These were: Alderman Johnson, Councillor Burtinshaw, Councillor James Needham (not present), George Walthew (not present), Jonathon Noden, William Bell, Thomas Meadows (not present), Samuel Kershaw, George Chatterton (not present), Francis Hornbuckle, and Benjamin Tidswell. George Walthew was probably one of the partners in John & George Walthew, cotton spinners and doublers who then operated Brinksway, Wellington and Spring Mount Mills in Stockport. Thomas Meadows was probably one of the partners in T. & W. Meadows, building contractors of Heaton Norris, who acted as building contractors for the mill.

The provisional directors were to prepare a prospectus which was duly published on 4 July 1884, although the company had not at that date been registered. There had been a considerable reshuffle as only six of the original eleven appear as provisional directors and a seventh completely new name appears.[24] These are: William Bell, Councillor Burtinshaw, James Goodall, Francis Hornbuckle, Alderman Johnson, Jonathon Noden and Benjamin Tidswell. Alderman Johnson had been appointed chairman rather than Councillor Burtinshaw. William Smith had been replaced by William Charlesworth as solicitor, and it was his address, Warren Street Chambers, Warren Street, Stockport, which was given as the registered office.

Stott & Sons of Manchester and Oldham had now been appointed as architects and had surveyed the existing premises, assuring the directors that the convertible parts were worth more than double the £4500 which had been paid for the whole premises. The property had the right to free use of water from the River Goyt and they could use the existing tunnels for conveying water from the river. The existing chimney, boiler house, Green's economiser and offices would be re-used while the warehouse would be let or sold. Their plans had now been firmed up and they were to build a fireproof mill fronting Mersey Street containing about 70 000 mule spindles, the machinery to be of the most modern construction. This would leave room for a second mill of about the same size to be built fronting Queen Street. The idea of ring spinning had not been abandoned and it was suggested that the existing fireproof mill on the site, which

23 'Cotton Spinning in Stockport - Proposed new companies in Portwood and Heaton Norris', *Stockport Advertiser*, 30/5/1884, 7e-f.

24 Prospectus of the Palmer Mills Co.Ltd, *Stockport Advertiser*, 4/7/1884, 1c.

would not be taken down at present, was suitable for holding around 35 000 ring spindles. The concept of ring spinning was still sufficiently novel and controversial for them to mount a defence of this proposal, pointing out that two limited liability ring spinning concerns in Rochdale had paid dividends of 10 to 15 per cent for a number of years past while the system had been successfully adopted by a number of private spinners. They spoke of the cheapness of building material, labour and machinery, claiming it would cost 'considerably less than £1 per spindle'.

However, it was one thing to issue a share prospectus but quite another to get people interested. The capital of the company was to be £100 000 in 20 000 £5 shares and the intention was not to proceed until 5000 shares had been taken up. Applications for shares were to be made to the office of the secretary, William Charlesworth, at Warren Street Chambers and were to be accompanied by a deposit of 2s 6d.[25] A meeting was held at the Court House on the evening of Friday 18 July 1884 to give publicity to the company and all subscribers of 100 shares or more were invited to attend meetings of the provisional board.[26] The company was eventually registered on 11 September 1884 and a meeting was held at the Mechanics Institute on the following Wednesday to decide whether to go ahead or not in view of the fact that only 4259 shares had been taken, somewhat short of the original target of 5000. A series of letters published in the *Stockport Advertiser* on 12 September urging people to support the project made clear that its future was considered to be in the balance. However, despite not having reached the target number of shares, the meeting decided to go ahead.[27]

The Memorandum & Articles of Association, dated 10 September 1884, list the first directors with their addresses and occupations:

Name	**Address**	**Occupation**
William Bell	Belmont Terrace, Brinnington.	Pork Butcher.
John Burtinshaw	The Bower House, Heaton Norris.	Tin Plate Worker.
James Goodall	Broomfield Villa, Broomfield Road, Heaton Chapel.	Tailor and woollen draper.
Francis Hornbuckle	Norfolk Villa, Stepping Hill, Stockport.	Gentleman.
John Goode Johnson	Brinnington House, Stockport.	Calico Bleacher.
Jonathon Noden	Lord Street, Stockport.	Grocer and provision dealer.
Benjamin Tidswell	Osborne Terrace, Brinnington.	Gentleman.

John Goode Johnson is named as chairman. All these were local men but none of them, apparently, had any current involvement in cotton spinning. This was not uncommon and they would have relied on professional managers, who had worked their way up through the cotton industry, for day to day running of the mill. The description of John Burtinshaw as 'tin plate worker' might suggest that he came from the working classes but we can be fairly certain that he was a master, not an operative, tin plate worker.

The first available shareholders list is dated 23 January 1885 and by this date 4748 shares had been issued to 194 shareholders. This is an average holding of 24·5 shares. The distribution of numbers of shares held was as follows:

25 Public Notices - 'The Palmer Mills Co.Ltd.', *Stockport Advertiser*, 8/8/1884, 1c (repeated in following weeks).

26 Advertisement - 'The Palmer Mills Co.Ltd.', *Stockport Advertiser*, 18/7/1884, 1a.

27 TNA BT31/14779/20252 Palmer Mills Co.Ltd (Company registration file, all following information on shares and capital is taken from this source). Public Notice - 'The Palmer Mills Co.Ltd.', *Stockport Advertiser*, 12/9/1884, 1a. Letters - 'The Palmer Mills Co.Ltd.', *Stockport Advertiser*, 12/9/1884, 7e. 'Cotton Spinning in Stockport - The Palmer Mills Venture', *Stockport Advertiser*, 19/9/1884, 7e.

No. of Shares	No. of Persons	No. of Shares	No. of Persons
300	1	12	2
150	1	11	1
100	17	10	55
60	1	8	3
50	15	6	4
40	4	5	28
30	2	4	6
25	4	3	2
20	31	2	14
15	1	1	2

The directors all held 100 shares, but the largest shareholder with 300 shares was Joseph Leigh, of Bank Hall, Heaton Mersey, described as 'cotton spinner'. He was one of the partners in J. & T.Leigh who occupied a complex of mills to the north of Great Portwood Street, bordering the River Tame, which had recently been expanded with the addition of the large Meadow Mill. They must not have seen the newcomer as a threat to their existing business which specialised in the production of hosiery, that is knitting, yarns and were spinning worsted as well as cotton. Notable amongst the shareholders are the three partners in the architects Stott & Sons, each holding 50 shares. The partners in Stott & Sons were often actively involved in mill company promotion, but in this instance they seem to have been brought in later rather than being involved with the initial promotion. However, the building contractors, T. & W. Meadows do appear to have been involved during the promotion of the company, as has already been noted.

No one person, or group of persons, dominated the list of shareholders but there were a large number of small shareholders, 114 persons, that is 59%, holding 10 or fewer shares. The 'Oldham Limiteds' of the 1870s had been proclaimed as examples of working-class cooperation with many working people taking shares. Thomas Bruce at the meeting of 26 May 1884 held to consider the proposed mill in Heaton Norris, had proclaimed: 'The great capitalists of the country were the working classes - the originators of all capital - and if the working classes would only combine, which was the true essence of co-operation, these mills would multiply'. However, none of the people involved in the promotion of Palmer Mill can be regarded as working class. The wide range of occupations given in the first list of shareholders can be seen in the Appendix. Many of these descriptions are ambiguous, for example, 'cotton spinner' would normally be a master, not an operative, cotton spinner. However, the impression is that the majority of shareholders would most accurately be described as being from the middle classes with a considerable number of small businessmen. The categories of card nailer, carder, cotton operative, engine driver, overlooker, piecer, roller coverer, self-actor minder and servant are unambiguously working class but these constitute only 15 shareholders. These are all skilled workers, none held more than ten shares and some held only two. The piecer, James William Booth, has the same address as one of the self-actor minders, James Booth, so were probably father and son. Twenty-three shareholders were women, 11% of the total. The four organisations who held shares were the local Spinners & Twiners Association, that is the spinner's trade union; the Azelia Lodge Free Gardeners; the Vine Lodge 144 United Free Gardeners and the Stockport Industrial & Equitable Co-Operative Society, who held 60 shares. The Free Gardeners were a Friendly Society.[28] There were also three children each holding 2 shares, all members of the Stansfield family of Cobden Villas, Carrington Road, Stockport. Ernest and Emma were described as 'at school' while James appears as a 'minor'.

All but 19 persons were local to Stockport. Of these, nine were from Manchester, three from Liverpool, two from Hyde and one each from Oldham, Southport, Chester, Sheffield and Worthing in Sussex. One of those from Liverpool was a cotton broker and it is common to find Liverpool cotton brokers holding shares in spinning companies. He may have been hoping to get the job of being the companies cotton broker or it may already have been agreed that he should be. The only really distant shareholder was the one from Worthing in Sussex, the Rev.Joseph Lancaster of Holy Trinity Vicarage who held 30 shares. How he came to be a shareholder must be a matter of speculation but maybe he had relatives in Stockport. The one shareholder from Oldham was in fact Abraham Henthorn Stott, senior, of the architects Stott & Sons who, having largely retired from the business, gave his home address while his two sons, Jesse Ainsworth Stott and Abraham Henthorn Stott, junior, gave the Manchester office address. As far as is known, Palmer Mill was the first mill in Stockport to be designed by Stott & Sons, but later they came to have considerable involvement in the Stockport cotton industry. Jesse Ainsworth Stott moved to live in

[28] See en.wikipedia.org/wiki/Order_of_Free_Gardeners (accessed 17/12/2016).

Broomfield Road, Heaton Chapel in 1890 and then in 1895 built a house 'Greystead' at Heaviley on the Buxton Road heading south out of Stockport.[29] He lived here until his death in 1917. Later this house became part of the Acton Court Hotel, but was demolished in 2010 and a nursery school now occupies the site.

If the working classes made any contribution at all to the capital of these companies, it was as loanholders rather than shareholders. The 'Oldham Limiteds' developed a practice of only partially calling up shares and inviting loans from the public, via advertisements in the local press, to make up the rest of the capital and Palmer adopted this method of raising capital. That the future of the project was still not assured is suggested by the fact that the first advertisement inviting money to be deposited on loan at 4% interest per annum did not appear in the *Stockport Advertiser* until 1 May 1885.[30] These advertisements appear regularly for the next month and then stop, starting again on 31 July 1885 when the rate of interest has been increased to 5%, suggesting difficulties in attracting capital leading them to offering a higher rate of interest.[31] The people of Stockport seem to have been more wary of investing their money in this way than were the people of Oldham.

---

29 Holden, *Stott & Sons*, 30.

30 Public Notices, *Stockport Advertiser*, 1/5/1885, 1a.

31 Public Notices, *Stockport Advertiser*, 31/7/1885, 1b.

Fig.12 The three partners in Stott & Sons, the architects for Palmer No.1 & 2 Mills. Top, the founder, Abraham Henthorn Stott with his two eldest sons, bottom left, Jesse Ainsworth Stott and, bottom right Abraham Henthorn Stott, junior. From a photograph taken for the Golden Wedding of Abraham Henthorn Stott in 1901/2.

Photograph courtesy of P.N.Stott.

Fig.13 'Greystead', 187 Buxton Road, Stockport. This house was built by Jesse Ainsworth Stott in 1895 and he lived here until he died in 1917; it was demolished in 2010.

N
SWANN STREET
LANCASTER STREET
QUEEN STREET
Mersey House
MERSEY STREET
Weighing Machine
GAS WORKS
Old Mill
No.1 Mill
VERNON MILLS
Engine House
Chimney
No.2 Mill
Boiler House
Engine House
RIVER GOYT
Foot Bridge
PALMER MILLS, STOCKPORT
BLOCK PLAN - 1893
0
100ft
0
50m
Approx. scales only
Derived from 1:1056 Ordnance Survey of Stockport,1895 edition, surveyed 1893, Sheet 6.

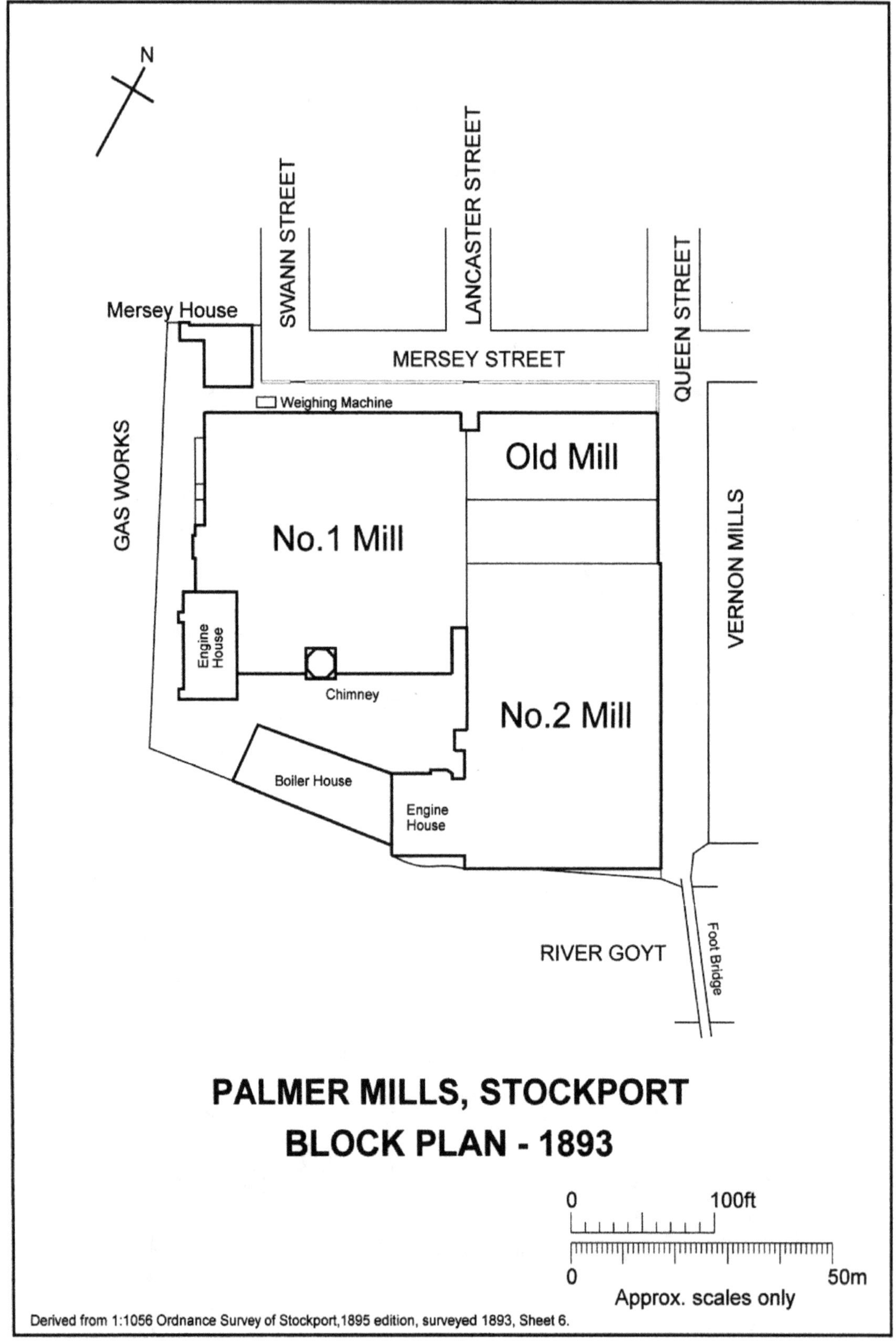

Fig.14

4. CONSTRUCTION OF THE No.1 MILL

Problems in raising capital appear to have slowed progress on the mill, although they did have to demolish parts of the old mills first. This consisted of buildings on the western half of the site, mainly blocks D and F; the eastern parts of the site, blocks A and B, were not demolished until the first mill was completed and they were ready to proceed to building the second mill. There is no evidence to suggest when this was done or how long it took, but it was not until the 27 June 1885 that the architects, Stott & Sons, inserted an advertisement in the *Oldham Chronicle* inviting tenders '...for the whole or any part of the works (except foundations and ironwork)...'.[32] This implies that by this date the contracts for demolition and putting in the foundations had already been let. As the contract went to T. & W. Meadows, who were involved in promotion of the company, advertising for tenders may have been little more than a formality and we may surmise that they had carried out the demolition and put in the new foundations. A further advertisement inviting tenders for the steam engines, boilers and millwrights work appeared on 8 August 1885.[33]

The building regulation plans were passed on 4 September 1885, although some of the submitted plans bear dates in June and July of that year.[34] There may have been problems getting these passed as there is an additional plan of the roving shed privies dated 3 September with a covering letter from Stott & Sons. However, failure to pass the building regulation plans had, legally or otherwise, not stopped them starting work as a cornerstone laying ceremony had been held on the previous Saturday, 29 August 1885.[35] The exact location of this cornerstone is not known, but at the almost contemporary Peel No.1 Mill, Bury, it was laid at one corner of the building, some 3 feet above ground level.[36] The implication is that by this date the foundations of the mill had been completed, together with the lower courses of brickwork. The cornerstone was, according to the *Oldham Chronicle* laid 'amid general rejoicing' and the people of Portwood 'hailed the proceedings with no little importance'. The ceremony took place at half past three in the afternoon and was performed by the Mayor of Stockport, Joseph Leigh, who was accompanied on the platform by the chairman of the company, Alderman Johnson, and by Daniel Adamson. Joseph Leigh, we have already noted, had a considerable shareholding in the company and was a partner in the firm of J. & T. Leigh. The engineer Daniel Adamson does not appear to have been a shareholder; although he was at one time a Stockport resident he then lived at The Towers, Didsbury, being at the height of his fame as chairman of the Manchester Ship Canal Company whose Act of Parliament had been granted Royal Assent earlier in that month. Joseph Leigh was also a director of the Ship Canal Company and no doubt Daniel Adamson was invited as a prominent public figure who would lend credibility to the enterprise. Jesse Ainsworth Stott was present as representative of the architects, Stott & Sons, and it was he who presented the silver trowel to Joseph Leigh for carrying out the ceremony while a mallet and square was presented to him by Mr. Meadows the building contractor. In handing over the silver trowel Jesse Ainsworth Stott made the rather barbed comment that he was pleased to see a partner in a private firm taking an active part because at one time private spinners looked upon companies in a very different light. Although there is no evidence that they were involved in the promotion of Palmer, Jesse would have been aware that the role of architects, and other contractors, in promoting spinning companies was controversial.

Progress of building work was marked by a number of accidents. On 14 May 1886 the *Stockport Advertiser* reported an accident to one of the workmen at the mill, Martin Kennedy of Hillgate, Stockport, who slipped when carrying a plank across girders on the fifth floor and fell 15 feet to the fourth floor, resulting in him being taken to the Stockport Infirmary.[37] Three weeks later another accident proved fatal when, on Friday, 4 May 1886, John Kennedy, of Cross Street, Stockport, was hit by a falling plank when he was standing by the hoist on the fourth floor.[38] One wonders if the two people in these accidents were related in any way. The Coroner's jury returned a verdict of accidental death but one of the jury observed that there had already been several accidents at the mill.

---

32 Public Notices, *Oldham Chronicle*, 27/6/1885, 4f.

33 Public Notices, *Oldham Chronicle*, 8/8/1885, 8f.

34 See listing of plans under 'Documentary Sources'.

35 'Palmer Mills Company, Stockport - Laying of the Cornerstone', *Oldham Chronicle*, 5/9/1885, 6c.

36 Holden, *Stott & Sons*, 175. This stone was laid on 15 August 1885.

37 'Awkward Fall at the Palmer Mills', *Stockport Advertiser*, 14/5/1886, 8f.

38 'The Fatal Accident at Palmer Mills', *Stockport Advertiser*, 11/5/1886, 7c.

The reports of these accidents clearly indicate that the brick-arch flooring of the fifth floor had not been completed at that date although the iron framework had been, together with flooring of the lower floors. Compared with other mills constructed around this time, this does represent slow progress and probably points to continuing difficulties in raising capital. For example, at the Granville Spinning Company, Oldham, the building contract had been let in May 1884 and by mid-July the following year the engine was reported to be ready to start and machinery was being installed in the mill. This machinery had been ordered in April and June 1884, around the time the building contract had been let, while the machinery for Palmer Mill was not ordered until the end of July 1886, ten months after the ceremonial laying of the cornerstone and when construction was well advanced.[39] By the end of June 1886 6182 shares had been taken up on which a total of £3022 17s 6d had been paid but this was greatly exceeded by the £17 616 0s 9d which had been deposited in loans, giving a total capital paid of £20 638 18s 3d.[40] This is a long way short of the £52 500 they would need to complete a mill of 70 000 spindles at 15s per spindle. At this date payments of £22 897 18s 7d had been made, £17 343 0s 8d of which was for the new building, suggesting that a considerable bank overdraft had been arranged.

The *Stockport Advertiser*'s 'Review of 1886', published on the last day of the year, stated that the new mill was approaching completion and it was expected to spin the first yarn in the first quarter of the new year, 1887.[41] This expectation was not quite achieved because the engine was not run for the first time until Monday, 4 April, with cotton starting to go through the mill on the following day. A manger had been appointed, John Eastwood who was previously with the Woodstock Spinning Company of Oldham.[42] All the machinery had not been installed by this date but it was usual practice to start work as soon as there was sufficient machinery. A month previously the meeting of shareholders had been held in the No.2 Spinning Room which was evidently still empty.[43]

At the following shareholders meeting on the 28 May 1887 the board were able to report that 28 000 pounds of cotton had been spun.[44] Issued share capital amounted to £7569 while the loan account stood at £33 091 1s 9d and £3443 7s 3d had been raised through sale of old materials, totalling £44 103 9s which still fell short of what would be needed to pay for the mill. However, the mill was now well and truly in business, three years after the first proposal of the project. To mark this fact the traditional ceremonial starting of the engines was performed on Wednesday 29 June 1887, the Mayor of Stockport, Joseph Leigh, performing the honours as he had done for the stone laying ceremony two years earlier.[45] In the presence of a large company of persons, including 'half a dozen ladies', the Mayor started the engines which were then christened with champagne 'Industry' and 'Perseverance' by the chairman Alderman Johnson. The most common practice was to name engines after wives and daughters of the directors but here they adopted names with a moral. Clearly this was a matter of civic pride and interest as no fewer than fifteen aldermen and councillors were present plus five Justices of the Peace. Also present were representatives of the various contractors to the mill. Mr.Stott represented the architects but the report does not say if this was Jesse Ainsworth Stott or younger brother Abraham Henthorn Stott, junior. Both Mr. T and Mr. W. Meadows, the building contractors were present, as were Mr. T. Oldham who made the boilers, Mr. Dixon representing Musgrave & Company who made the engines, Mr. J. Elce representing Lord Brothers who made the blowing room machinery and Mr. Clegg representing Asa Lees who made the spinning machinery. The usual self congratulatory speeches and toasts followed. The chairman repeated his belief that it was one of the cheapest mills in the country and said that 8000 shares had been taken up but if they could increase this to 12 000 then they could complete the mill with only £2 10s called up per share.

---

39 The machinery for both Palmer and Granville Mills was ordered from Asa Lees & Co.Ltd. of Oldham and can be traced in their production records held by the Lancashire Archives, Preston. Orders for Palmer Mill are detailed under 'Documentary Sources' at the end of this study. Orders for Granville Mill are: DDPSL/4/5/1 Mule Order Book 1883-1885, pg.152-3, 12 June 1884; DDPSL/4/4/3 Slubbing, Intermediate and Roving Frames Order Book 1883-1885, pg.132-134, 17 April 1884.

40 'Palmer Mills Co.Ltd.', *Stockport Advertiser*, Friday, 27/8/1886, 5f. This article gives the statement of accounts for the quarter ended 30 June 1886.

41 'Review of 1886', *Stockport Advertiser*, 31/8/1886, 6c.

42 'Starting of Palmer Mills', *Stockport Advertiser*, 8/4/1887, 5f. 'Palmer Mills, Stockport', *Oldham Chronicle*, Saturday, 16/4/1887, 8e.

43 'Palmer Mills Company, General Meeting', *Stockport Advertiser*, 4/3/1887, 8f.

44 'Palmer Mills Company, General Meeting', *Stockport Advertiser*, 3/6/1887, 3g.

45 'Palmer Mills Company, Engines Started by the Mayor', *Stockport Advertiser*, 1/7/1887, 7c-d. This refers to a full description of the mill having appeared previously but this could not be located.

The mill was not fully equipped and working at this date. At the next quarterly meeting on Saturday, 20 August 1887 it was reported that some 43 000 spindles were at work.[46] Nevertheless, they were able to declare a profit of £72 11s 9d for the quarter, which was to be carried forward. It was resolved to adopt the 'Oldham style' of balance sheet and Councillor Burtinshaw thought that the starting of No.2 mill should not long be delayed, even though only 7622 of the 20 000 shares had been taken. By the next quarterly meeting on Wednesday 2 November 1887 60 000 spindles, two-thirds of the total were at work and it was hoped that all the machinery would be installed and working by the end of the year.[47] A profit of £320 6s 1d was declared for the quarter which gave a total of £392 17s 6d when combined with that for the previous quarter and it was decided to award a dividend of 4% which left a balance of £96 19s 6d. William Helm retired as a director at this meeting, he did not seek re-election and no replacement was appointed, leaving six directors. On the previous Saturday, 29 October 1887, a workpeople's tea-party and *soiree* had been held at the Mechanics' Institute to inaugurate completion of the mill.[48] 350 people, including 230 workpeople, were present and speeches referred to the hope to complete No.2 Mill.

Completion of the mill had taken rather longer than its competitors in Oldham. Granville Mill, mentioned above, had taken little more than 16 months from inception of the project and commencement of building to starting production. At Palmer it had taken 32 months from the inception of the project and 20 months from start of construction until production had commenced. Completion took a further eight months.

A mill of this size would have offered, in principle, new employment opportunities for local people. But in practice some of these people would need to be already experienced in the operations of a large modern mill and may not have been readily available in Stockport. In Oldham, where there had been a high rate of new mill building, it had become the practice for the mule spinners at a new mill to be recruited from big piecers, who were looking for promotion to mule spinner, at existing mills. But in Stockport there would not have been such a ready supply. A letter appeared in the *Stockport Advertiser* in June 1887 from John Prunty, secretary of the Stockport Operative Cotton Spinners and Twiners Association complaining that Stockport spinners had not been employed at Vernon Mill and that the same thing was happening at Palmer Mill.[49] He said that in 1880 he had an interview with 'a worthy gentleman who is now a director of the Palmer Mills Spinning [*sic*] Co.Ltd.' to see if they would agree to the use of the Oldham List in the new mills. This had been agreed to and as a result the Association had actively assisted in the promotion of Vernon by canvassing the town and encouraging the working classes to take up shares. But despite this he now found cause to complain that Stockport spinners were not being employed. The Oldham List referred to is the piece rate list for paying mule spinners and the Association was clearly concerned that the new mills should not try to undercut the Oldham mills by paying a lower piece rate.

As to the final cost of No.1 Mill, this was later stated to have been 19s (£0·95) per spindle, that is just under £75 000 in total and greater than the 15s originally hoped for. This included 5 cottages at the end of Swann Street at a cost of £1000, presumably the ones directly adjoining Mersey House which appear on the 1892 Ordnance Survey plan. It is unclear whether the company had built these cottages or simply purchased them. They are not on the 1872 Ordnance Survey. One shareholder queried this item saying that 'they did not generally spend £1000 on five cottages'.[50] The company retained ownership of Mersey House but not the warehouse on the opposite side of Mersey Street, between Swann Street and Lancaster Street. This is shown to have been demolished on the 1892 Ordnance Survey with the site vacant. It was still vacant in 1907 but a church had appeared by 1934; this was a short lived structure which had gone by 1960.

---

46 'Palmer Mills Company Quarterly Meeting', *Stockport Advertiser*, 26/8/1887, 7d. The report actually says 4300 spindles but this must be a misprint, as this would only be two pairs of mules.

47 'Palmer Mills Company; Retirement of a Director', *Stockport Advertiser*, 4/11/1887, 7g.

48 'The Palmer Mills Co.Ltd.', *Stockport Advertiser*, 4/11/1887, Supplement, 2c.

49 Letter 'Cotton Spinning in Stockport', *Stockport Advertiser*, 17/6/1887, 3g.

50 'Palmer Mills Meeting', *Stockport Advertiser*, 14/2/1890, 8d.

Fig.15 Architect's perspective view of No.1 Mill with the Old Mill to the left and Mersey House in front. This is evidently from a newspaper but the original has not been traced and this comes from a copy in the possession of the Stockport Heritage Trust. The incorrect date of 1881 has been added at some time. The rural foreground is clearly fanciful.

5. DESCRIPTION OF THE No.1 MILL

As shown on the block plan (fig.14), the No.1 Mill occupied the western part of the site, replacing blocks D and F of the old mills and also taking part of the garden of Mersey House. The architect's perspective view (fig.15) shows the mill from the north-west with the Old Mill to the left and Mersey House in the foreground. The main body of the mill was eight bays long by six deep giving overall dimensions of approximately 180 feet (54·9m) long, including the rope race, by 130 feet (39·6m) deep (fig.16). Including the cellar, it was six storeys and approximately 90 feet (27·4) high (fig.17). To the rear there was an extension to the ground floor and cellar, two bays and approximately 40 feet (12·2m) deep. The engine house was on the south-west corner of the mill, in line with the rope race which was on the west end of the mill. The positioning of the rope race at the end of the mill, although common after 1900, was unusual for this date as it was then normal practice for it to be internal to the mill, about a third of the way along. This arrangement is seen, for example, at the almost contemporary Chadderton Mill, Oldham.[51] One of the reasons for adopting this arrangement was because the opening, or blowing, room, which was most dangerous in terms of fire, could be installed in the short end of the mill and the rope race then formed a fire-wall between it and the rest of the mill. However, this consideration was not relevant at Palmer Mill because the blowing room was sited separately in a part of the Old Mill. Also the Palmer No.1 Mill was shorter, although one storey higher, than many contemporary mills and installing the rope race internally would not have been very satisfactory from this point of view.

The engine house was a lofty structure rising to the height of the first spinning room (fig.15 & 28), rectangular in plan with tall arched windows, five along the long side on two in the short side. The hipped roof had a prominent ventilator in the centre and decorative corner parapets echoed those on the body of the mill.

The staircase projected on the south-east corner of the mill. There was a hoist tower going the whole height of the mill in the centre of the south wall of the mill. The chimney was also on the south of the mill and its pedestal took up part of the extension. This somewhat unusual location for a chimney is explained by the fact that it was the old chimney reused. This chimney was octagonal, rising from a square pedestal; its height is not known with certainty but photographs suggest that it was about 200 feet (61m), which was typical for spinning mill chimneys. The boiler house was to the south, not attached to the mill, but ranged along the boundary wall with the river. Again this was a reuse of the old boiler house, although it would have been rebuilt to house the new boilers. The dust flue was on the north-east corner of the mill where the mill was connected to block C of the Old Mill which was retained.

The external walls of the mill were brick with stone dressings. Windows, two per bay in both directions, were arch headed. Compared with mills built after 1900, by Stott & Sons and other architects, the mill was a plain structure. Decorative work was confined to the roof parapets at the corners and also above the hoist. There was recessed panelling at the corners and between the windows on the top floor. Even this minimal decoration, particularly that over the hoist, was to cause comment by shareholders.

The mill was of fireproof construction following the system described in Patent 7967 of 1885 granted to the three partners in Stott & Sons. The Provisional Specification is dated 30 June 1885 and the Complete Specification 27 March 1886 which coincides with the commencement of work on Palmer No.1 Mill and, as far as is known, this was the first mill to be built following this Patent. The principles of this system can be seen from the isometric view of the iron work for a single bay (fig.18) and the patent drawings (fig.19 & 20). This system gave a bay which was, nominally, 21 feet (6·4m) square as against the previous single brick-arch system, as used in the Old Mill (fig.8 & 9), which gave bays of 10 feet 6 inches by 20 feet (3·2m by 6·1m). This reduced the number of columns and gave a clear span over a pair of mules. Mules were always arranged in pairs and in the single brick-arch system the area between the mules where the spinner and his piecers worked was obstructed by columns but the 21 foot bay left this area clear. Whether a concern for the spinners' working environment played any part in the development of the patent is unclear because this is not mentioned in the specification, which simply refers to the fact that there is no longer any risk of damage from skips or other articles being left so that they could be crushed between the mule carriage and a column. The cast iron columns supported double longitudinal main girders which were joined by transverse secondary girders at 5 foot 3 inch intervals. The main longitudinal girders were deep

[51] Roger N.Holden, *Chadderton Mill: the History of an Oldham Cotton Spinning Mill* (Stockport: Roger N.Holden, 2017).

enough to accommodate the brick arches; if a single girder had been used it would have needed to be much deeper which would have obstructed the light and interfered with the leather belting which drove the machinery.

The columns were of cast iron, although the patent specification permits of other materials. The girders were rolled I-sections. The patent specification allows them to be of '...cast, wrought or rolled iron or steel', but wrought iron by preference. We may take this as an indication that wrought iron would have been used here at Palmer No.1 Mill, particularly as rolled steel did not become generally available in Britain until 1886.[52] Before this wrought iron girders were largely supplied from Continental iron works, particularly in Belgium, and such may have been the source for Palmer Mill.[53] As for the actual floor material the patent specification allows a variety of materials '... brick arching, slabs or arches of concrete or other suitable fire resisting material.' The drawings show brick arches and in practice this was probably the only material used, as it was here at Palmer No.1 Mill. The patent drawings show the specially shaped bricks which fitted against the girders to form the root of the arch.

What the patent does not mention and the drawings do not show is what happens in the end bays where the girders meet the wall. The wall running parallel to the main girders had to support the ends of the secondary girders. These were supported on short sections of girder embedded into the wall and supported by the wall pillars (fig.22 & 60). In the other direction, at right angles to the main girders and parallel to the secondary girders, the brick arches and secondary girders were turned through 90 degrees in the end bays so that there was no outward thrust on the walls (fig.21). Note that in the corners it was impossible not to have an arch thrusting outwards but this was made as small as possible.

Dimensions for the girders at Palmer No.1 Mill are not known. Actual bay dimensions differed from the nominal 21 feet (fig.16). In the longitudinal direction the bays were 20 feet 6 inches (6·3m), except the two end bays which were larger, although the dimensions of the west end bay are not actually marked on the Building Regulation Plans from which this is taken. In the transverse direction they vary in an apparently random fashion from 18 feet 6 inches up to 23 feet 4 inches (5·6m to 7·1m).

The roof of Palmer No.1 Mill was a flat, tank, roof, following what was by then fairly standard Lancashire practice. The roof was formed in exactly the same way as the floors below, with brick arches levelled off with concrete. But instead of the concrete being covered by floor boards it was covered with a layer of asphalt which was also continued up the sides of the parapet which surrounded the roof. A six inch layer of water was then left permanently standing on this in order to protect the asphalt from the weather.

Mersey House, originally the Manager's house, was retained but was probably converted for use as offices, rather than remaining as a residence.

---

[52] Jonathan Clarke, *Early Structural Steel in London Buildings* (Swindon: English Heritage, 2014), 22.

[53] Clarke, *Early Structural Steel*, 18.

PALMER No.1 MILL, STOCKPORT
GROUND PLAN
Engine House
Rope Race
Chimney
Hoist
Wall of mill
Card Room
20'6"
20'6"
20'6"
20'6"
20'6"
20'6"
22'
23'4"
19'6"
21'
22'6"
23'
21'6"
22'
18'6"
Entrance
Staircase
Carders Room
Grinders Room
Passage
Dust Flue
Centre lines of columns
N
This is a sketch only and is partly conjectural.
Derived from Stott & Sons Drawing No.6172, 9 June 1885.

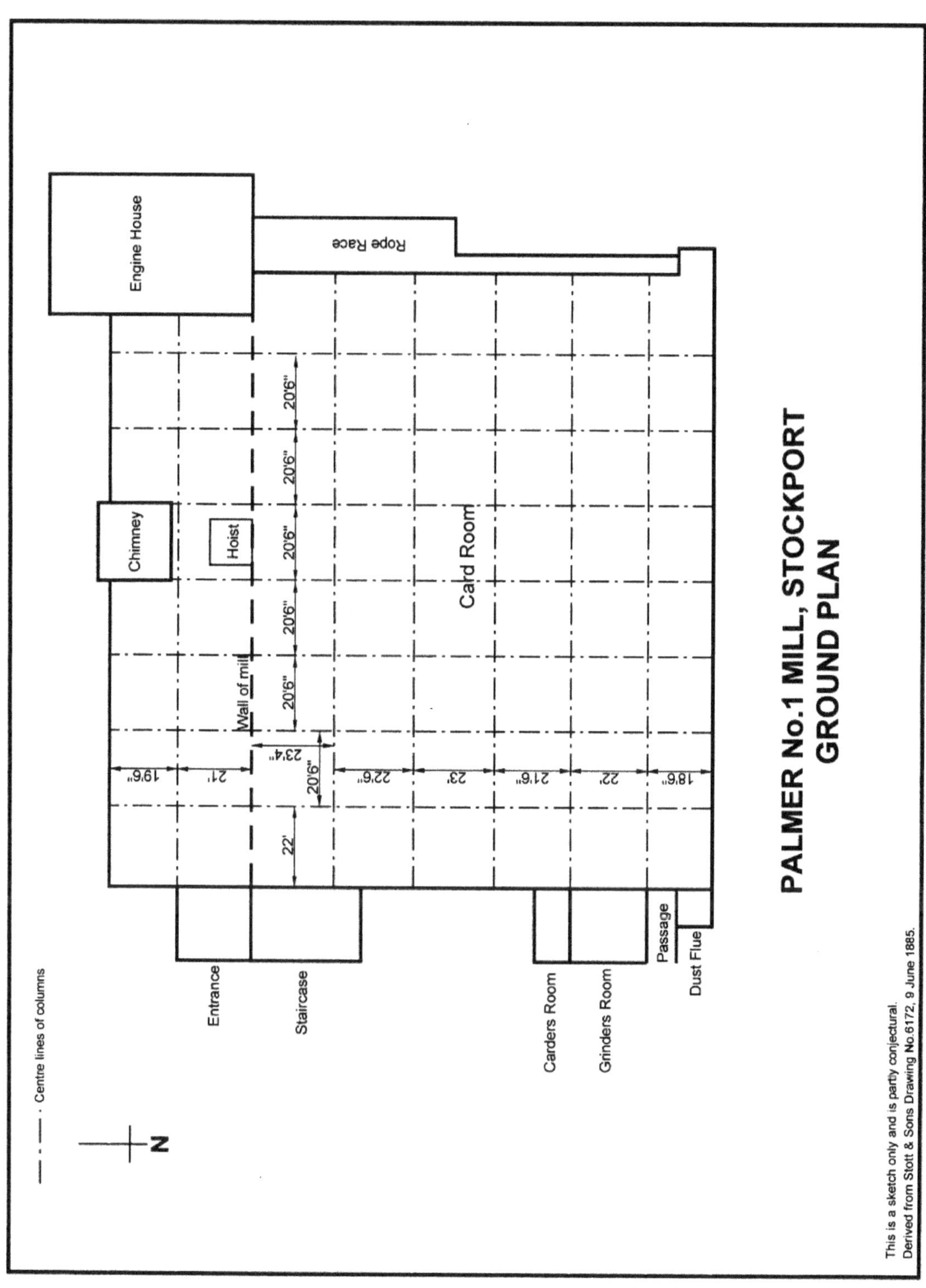

Fig.16

PALMER No.1 MILL, STOCKPORT
CROSS-SECTION
Warehouse
4th Spinning Room
3rd Spinning Room
2nd Spinning Room
1st Spinning Room
Card Room
Conditioning Cellar
This is a sketch only and is partly conjectural
Derived from Stott & Sons Drawing No.6212, 27 June 1885.

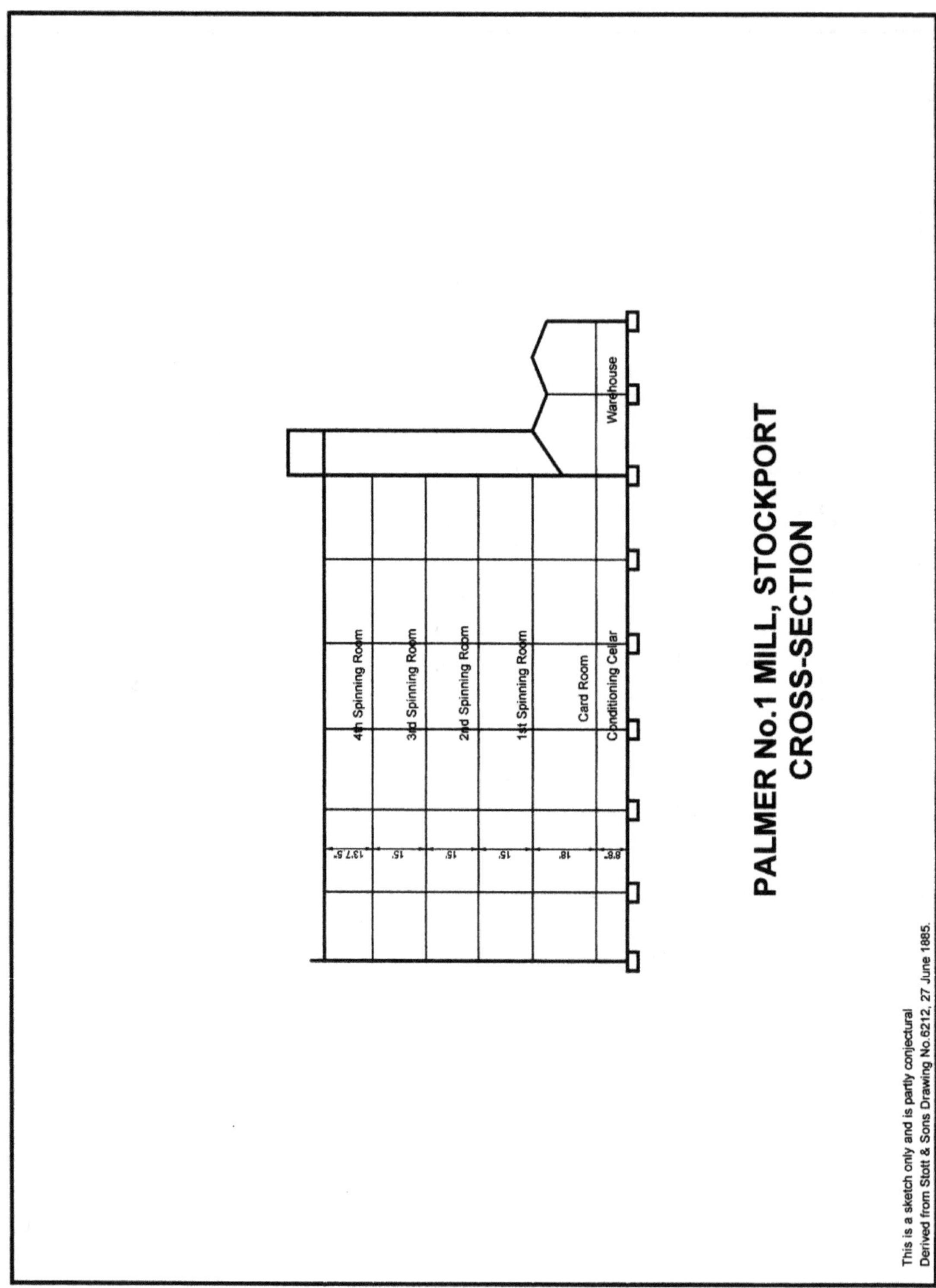

Fig.17

STOTT & SONS 1885 PATENT
FIREPROOF CONSTRUCTION
Isometric View

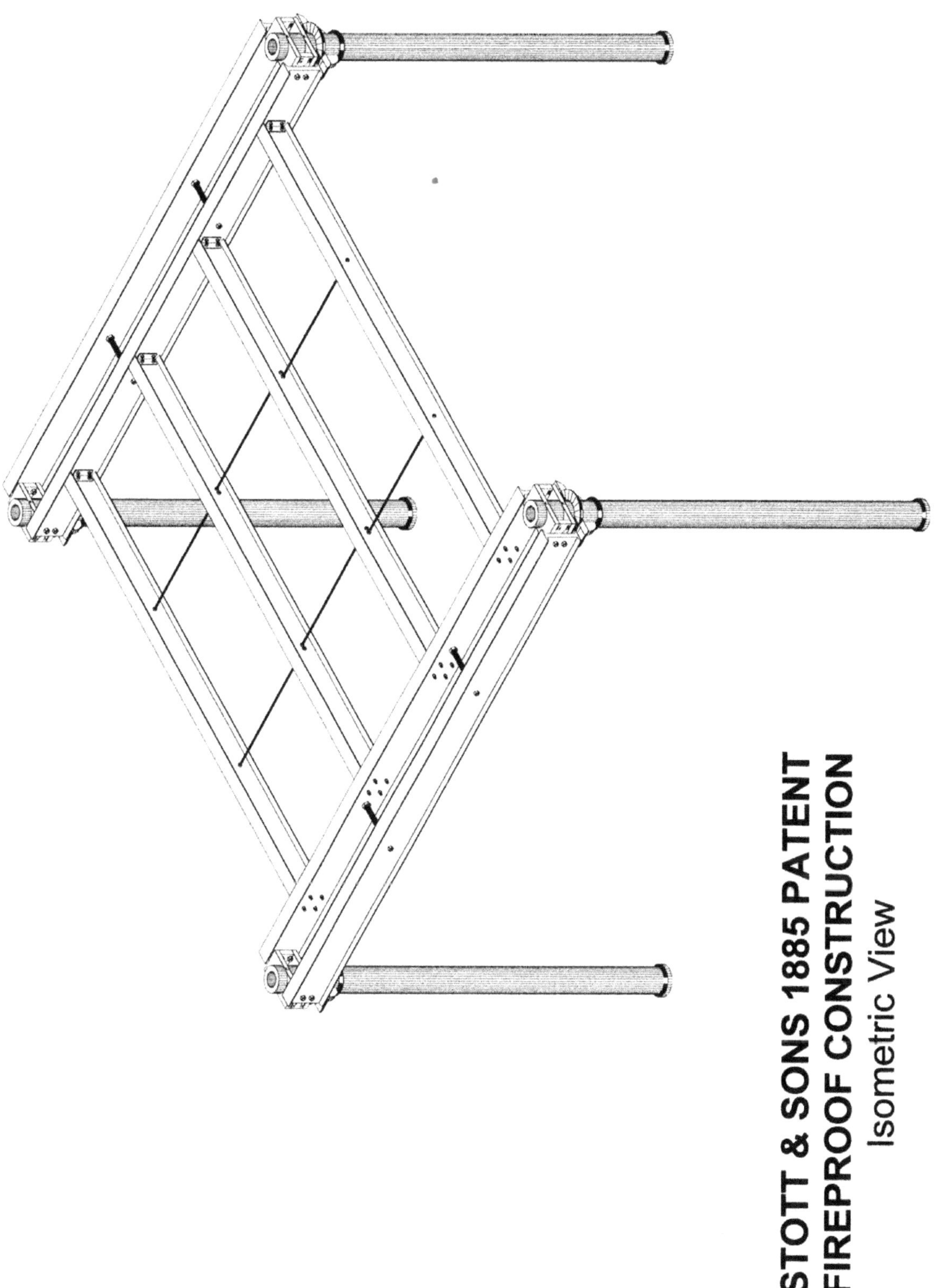

Fig.18

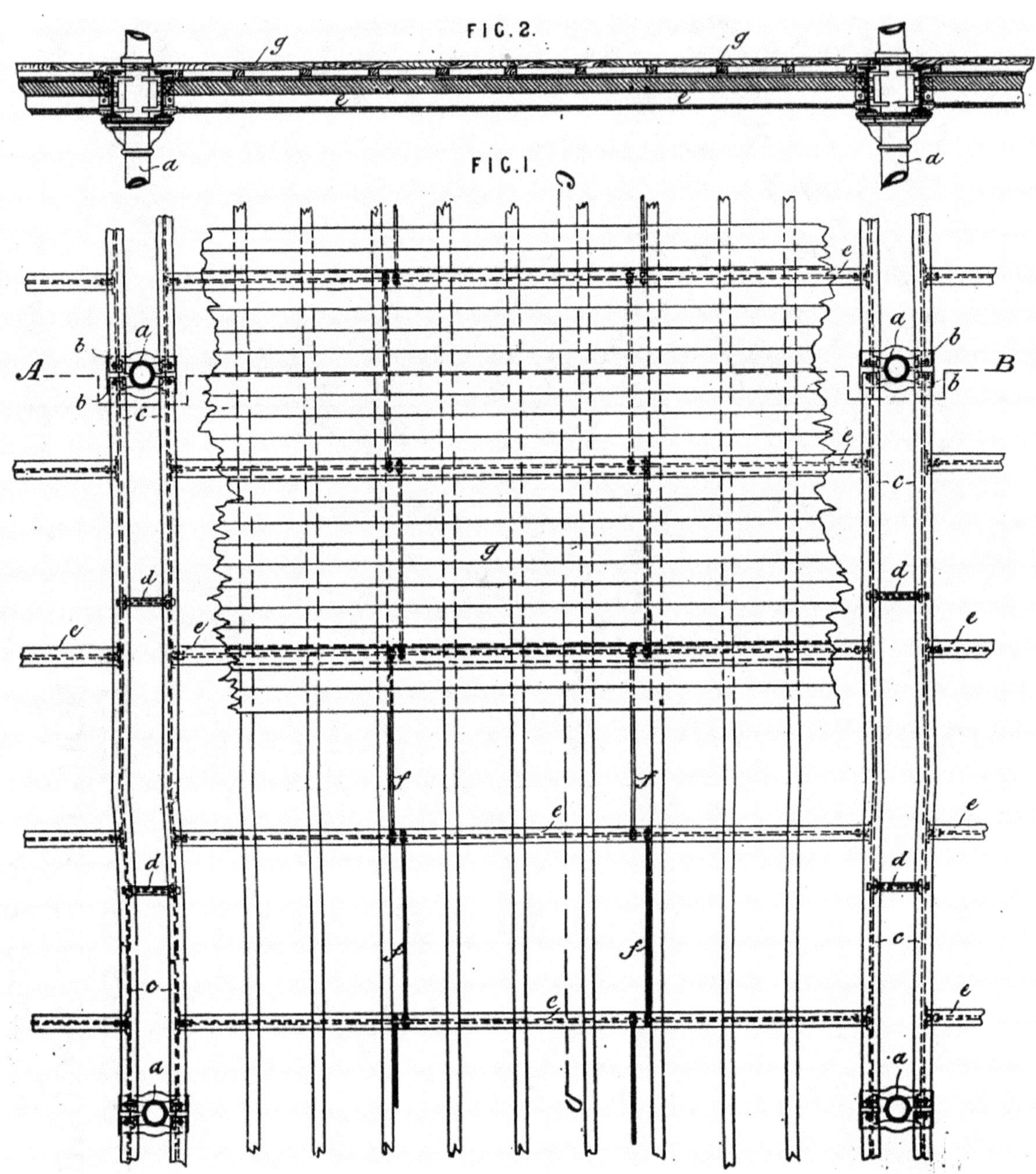

Fig.19 Drawings from Stott & Sons Patent No.7967 of 1885. Fig.1 is a plan view and fig.2 is a section on line AB.

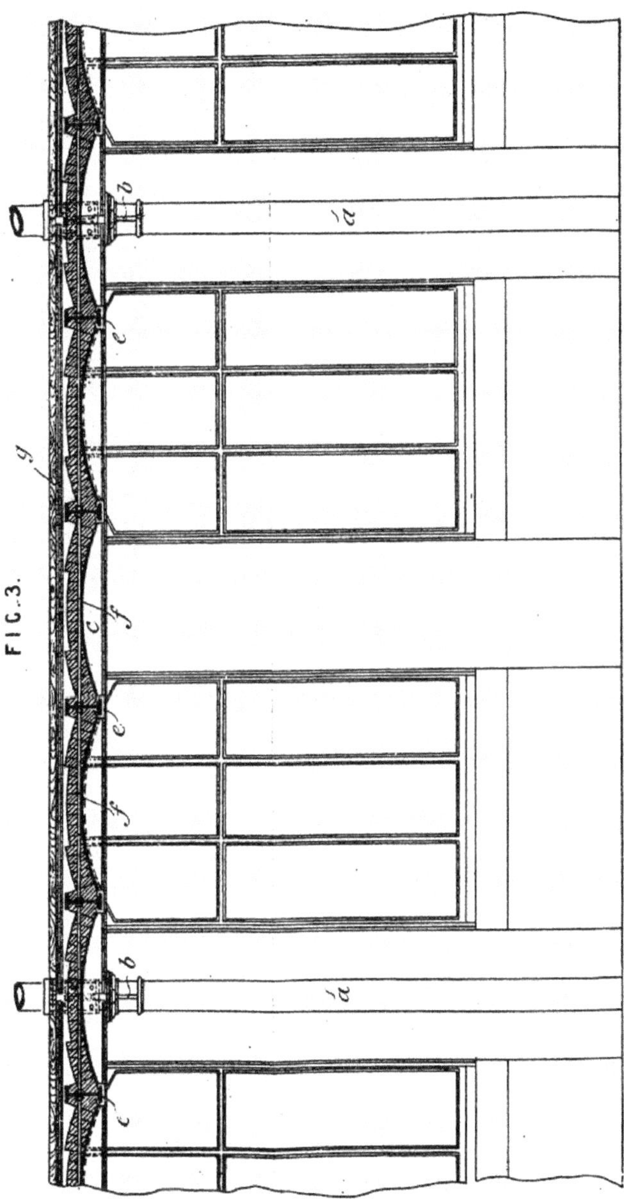

Fig.20 Drawing from Stott & Sons Patent No.7967 of 1885. Fig.3 is a section on line CD fig.1 (Fig.19).

Rope Race
PALMER No.1 MILL, STOCKPORT
GIRDER PLAN
Main Girders
Secondary Girders
Columns
Brick Arches

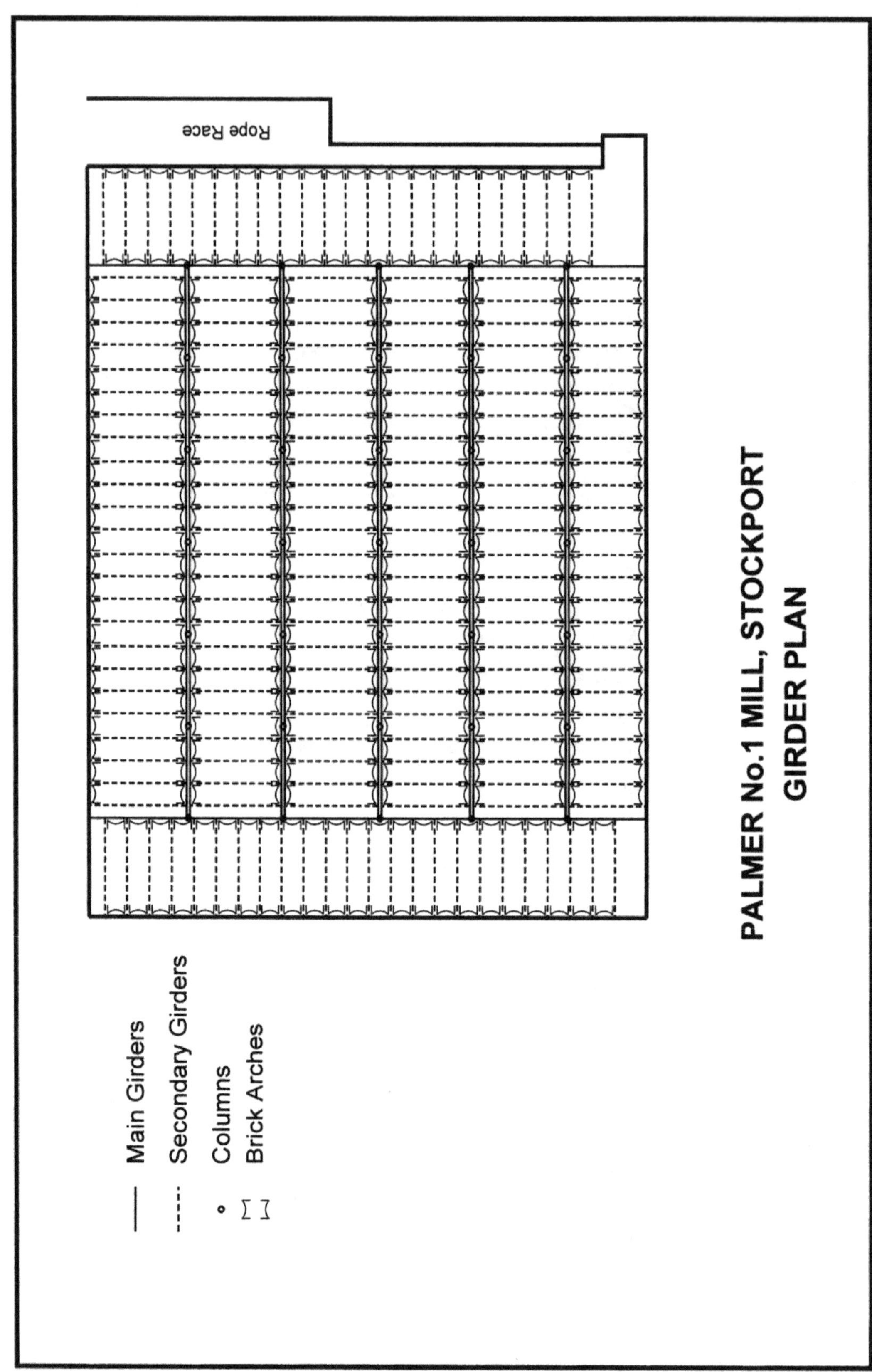

Fig.21

a) Elevation
Secondary girder
Connecting girder
Wall pier
b) Plan
DIAGRAM SHOWING
TERMINATION OF SECONDARY GIRDERS
AT THE WALL

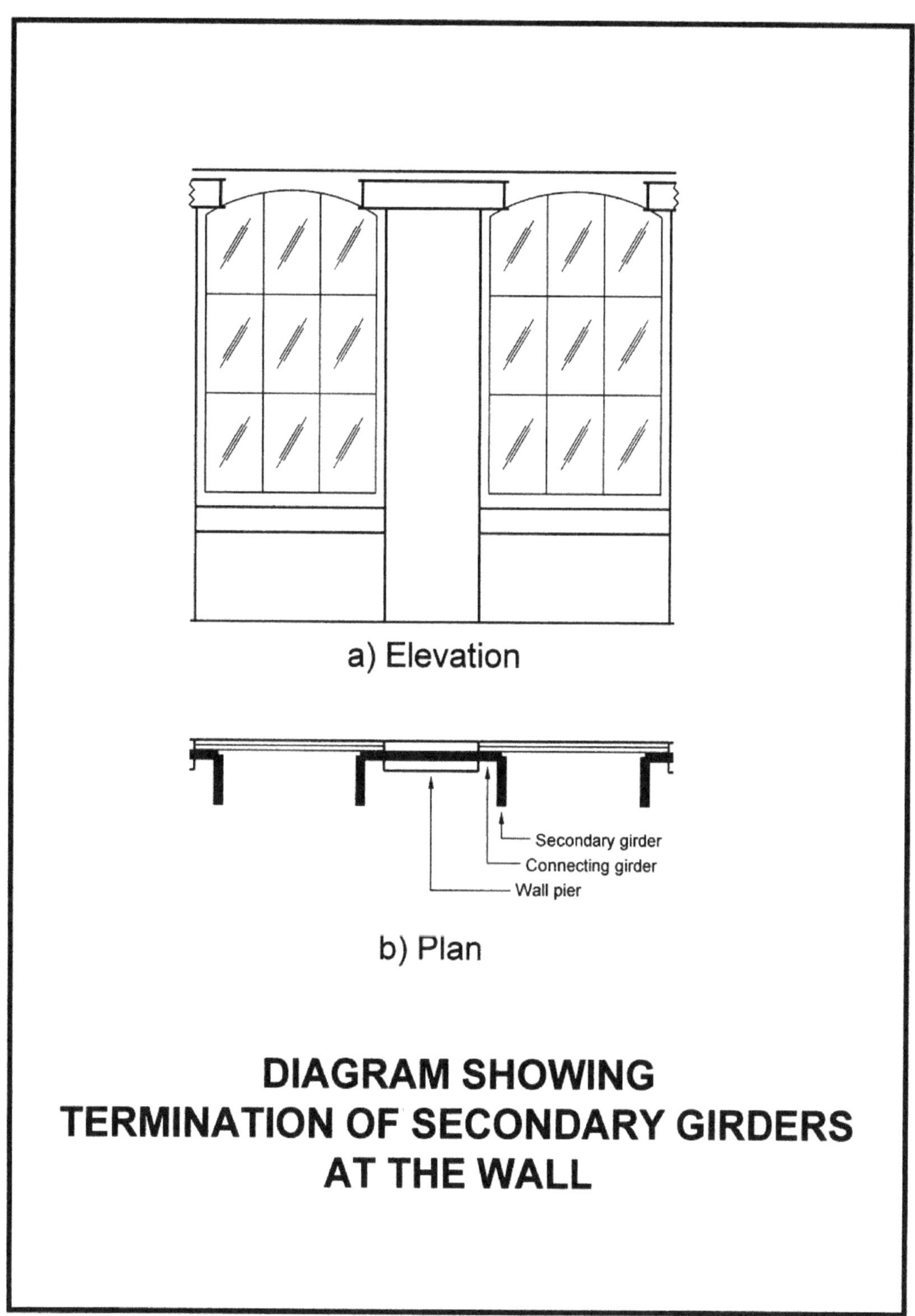

Fig.22

Rope Race
Gangway
Hoist
Centre lines of columns
Staircase
Pair of mules
PALMER No.1 MILL, STOCKPORT
MULE ROOM LAYOUT

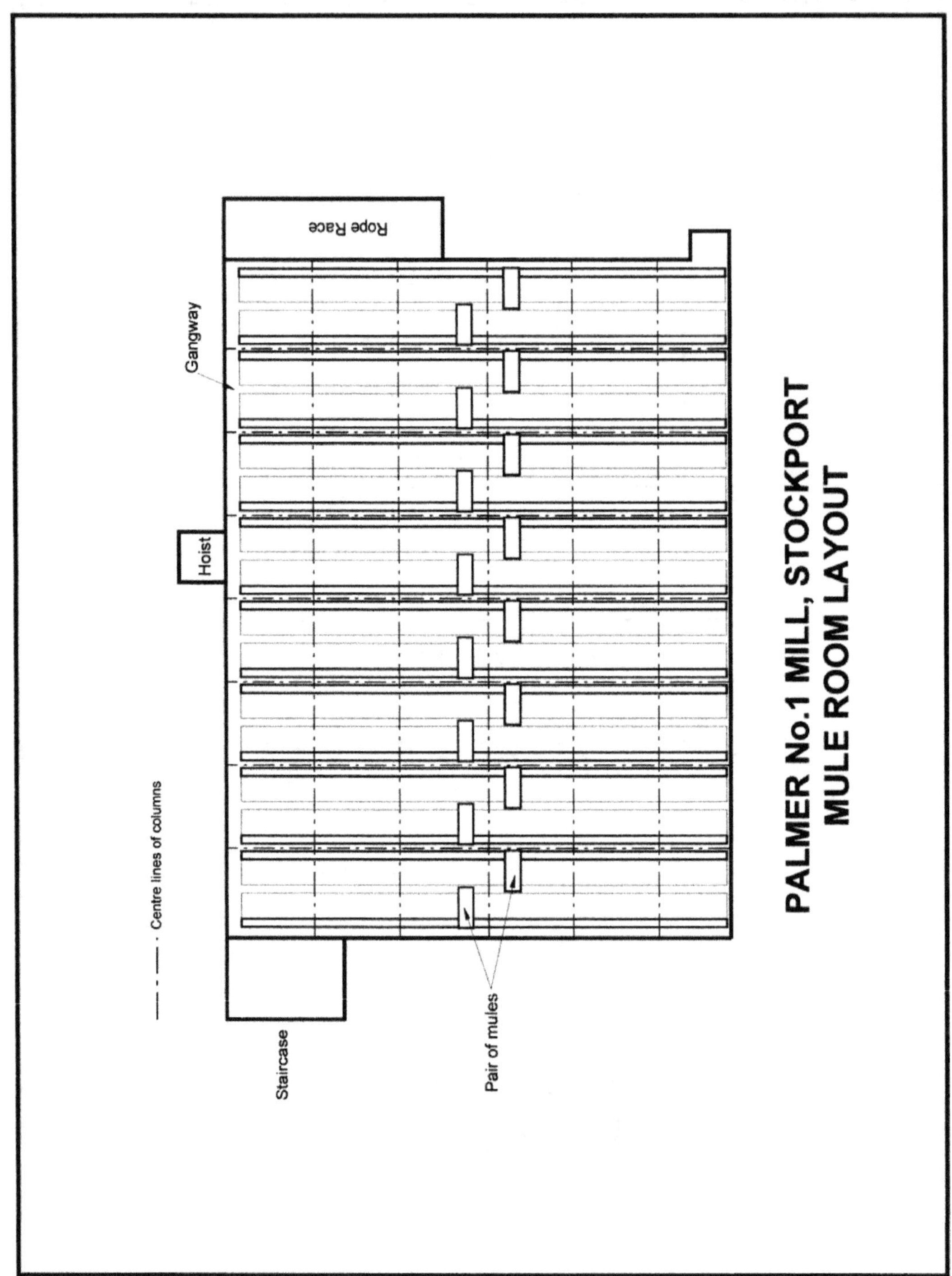

Fig.23

6. EQUIPMENT OF THE No.1 MILL

The processes at Palmer Mill were typical for cotton spinning mills at that date. There is not space here to describe these in detail. Although writing in the 1960s, and making some reference to later developments, Tippett provides a good introduction to the processes in cotton spinning mills.[54] In brief cotton came into the mill in highly compressed bales, which included quite a lot of impurities mixed in with the cotton fibre. First the bales had to be broken into smaller pieces which were then fed into the opening machines that started to separate the fibres and remove impurities. The output from the opening machines was fed to machines called scutchers which continued the process of separating the fibres and removing impurities, finally forming the cotton fibre into a lap, this is a loose sheet of fibre formed into a roll. Because fans were used in removing the impurities, the place where the openers and scutchers were located was commonly known as the blowing room. The impurities were removed to the dust cellar, which vented to atmosphere via the dust flue. The laps from the scutchers fed the carding engines. The carding engines separated the individual cotton fibres in the lap, removing any remaining impurities, and formed them into a loose continuous rope of fibre known as sliver. To even out irregularities, up to four slivers were then joined together in the draw, or drawing, frames. The next process was to form the sliver into roving for the actual spinning process. Production of roving involved drawing out the sliver into a much smaller diameter and lightly twisting it to hold it together. This was performed on machines known as speed frames, usually in three stages known respectively as slubbing, intermediate and roving frames. The place where all these machines from the carding engines to the roving frames were located was known as the card room.

The roving was wound onto bobbins for the final spinning process. Spinning consists in drafting, that is attenuating the roving to the required fineness, and twisting to mechanically bind the fibres together to form yarn. Finally the formed yarn has to be wound into a yarn package. Palmer Mill, in common with the majority of mills in Lancashire, used mules for spinning, but some mills used throstles or later ring frames. Mules were not all the same, but were constructed differently to spin either weft or twist yarn. Essentially, weft yarn was used, as its name implies, for the weft in weaving while twist was used for the warp. But spinners used these terms although not all yarn went for weaving. Some went for uses like thread, knitting or lace. For a spinner the essential difference between weft and twist was the direction of twist in the yarn and how hard it was twisted, that is the number of turns per inch put into the yarn. Weft was spun with the spindles running anti-clockwise and was soft spun, that is with fewer turns per inch. Twist was spun with the spindles running clockwise and was hard spun with more turns per inch to give strong yarns which could be used for warp. Very highly twisted yarns, however, were spun using throstles or later ring frames. Weft yarn was spun into smaller packages than twist so there was a greater density of spindles on weft mules. For mules, the standard was for the distance between the spindles, or gauge as it was called, to be 1⅛ inch (28·575mm) for weft and 1⅜ inch (34·925mm) for twist. The fineness of the yarn produced was denoted by count. The count was the number of hanks of yarn, 840 yards (768m) in length, which made up a weight of one pound (0·45kg). Thus, the higher the count the finer the yarn.

The mules spun yarn into a package known as a cop and the completed cops were passed into the conditioning cellar, where they were allowed to stand for some time in a damp atmosphere to regain moisture so the yarn was amenable for use. Finally they were passed to the warehouse for dispatch.

The large textile machinery manufacturers in Lancashire, such as Platt Brothers of Oldham and Dobson & Barlow of Bolton, would equip a whole mill. But there were also some smaller manufacturers who specialised in particular types of machinery so the whole of the machinery was not always ordered from the same suppler and this was the case for Palmer No.1 Mill.

The blowing room machinery was ordered from Thomas Lord of Todmorden, who specialised in this type of machinery, and consisted of:

2 cotton openers.
4 single beater intermediate scutchers.
4 finisher lap machines.

[54] L.H.C.Tippett, *A Portrait of the Lancashire Textile Industry* (London: Oxford University Press, 1969), 49-66.

This machinery was installed in the section of the Old Mill to the east of No.1 Mill.[55] It will be noted, however, that a dust flue is shown on the north-east corner of No.1 Mill (fig.16). Presumably this was built to serve the blowing room in the Old Mill. The layout in the Old Mill is not known, but contemporary practice would suggest a mixing room on the first floor feeding down to the scutchers and openers on the ground floor below. These in turn would have exhausted in to the dust chamber in the basement, which was connected to the dust flue.

The remainder of the machinery, consisting of the card room machinery and the actual spinning machinery, was ordered from Asa Lees & Company Limited of Oldham on the 27 July 1886.[56] The card room machinery consisted of:

64	double, roller and clearer, carding engines.	
15	draw frames.	4 heads of 4 deliveries each.[57]
9	slubbing frames, 96 spindles each.	864 spindles in total.
16	intermediate frames, 144 spindles each.	2304 spindles in total.
46	roving frames,	7544 spindles in total.
	consisting of:	
	4 of 176 spindles.	704 spindles in total.
	26 of 172 spindles.	4472 spindles in total.
	16 of 148 spindles.	2368 spindles in total.

The actual spinning machinery consisted of 64 mules, with 78 444 spindles in total, made up of:[58]

46	1⅛ inch gauge weft mules,	59 232 spindles in total.	
	consisting of:		
	16 of 1278 spindles.	20 448 spindles in total.	Length 125ft.
	16 of 1290 spindles.	20 640 spindles in total.	Length 126ft.
	14 of 1296 spindles.	18 144 spindles in total.	Length 126ft 6in.
18	1⅜ inch spindle gauge twist mules	19 212 spindles in total.	
	consisting of:		
	2 of 1062 spindles.	2124 spindles in total.	Length 126ft 6in.
	16 of 1068 spindles.	17 088 spindles in total.	Length 127ft.

The available records do not state what yarn counts these mules were designed to produce.

The suggestion of installing ring frames was not acted upon at this time and the mill was set up as a traditional mule spinning mill.[59] There is no indication of the intended markets for the yarn produced by the mill, whether or not it was all directed at the weaving market or for other purposes such as thread production. There was a notable imbalance between weft and twist spindles since 75·5 % were weft, the remaining 24·5% being twist. This imbalance of weft and twist was typical for Oldham mule spinning mills, some of which produced only weft yarn. This imbalance is explained by the fact that some cloths used throstle, and later ring, spun warp with mule spun weft while other cloths required more weft than warp. Throstle and ring spinning mills produced only twist.

---

55 This information on the opening machinery comes from the article 'Palmer Mills Company, Engines Started by the Mayor', *Stockport Advertiser*, 1/7/1887, 7c-d. No records for Thomas Lord have survived.

56 These orders can be found in the Asa Lees records held as part of the Platt-Saco-Lowell Archive at the Lancashire Record Office, Preston, and listed below under the heading 'Documentary Sources'.

57 Asa Lees' Draw Frame Order Book for this date does not survive but these are listed, along with the rest of the machinery, in the article 'Palmer Mills Company, Engines Started by the Mayor', *Stockport Advertiser*, 1/7/1887, 7c-d.

58 Lengths are given to the nearest 6in, allowing 5ft for the headstock and frame ends, the exact figure not being known for Asa Lees mules.

59 However, one report does mention 3072 ring spindles, but this seems to have been an error; it is possible that the reporter has confused some of the roving frames for ring frames (4 by 176 plus 16 by 148 spindles equals 3072). Holden, *Stott & Sons*, 224 is thus incorrect.

The mules would have been installed on the top four floors of the mill. The walls of the mill would have been narrower on the higher floors, giving a slightly wider floor space and advantage was taken of this to install longer mules on the higher floors. The top floor would house twist mules which had a greater spindle gauge. The next floor down would have housed the two twist mules of 1062 spindles and the 14 weft mules of 1296 spindles. On the floor below would have been the weft mules of 1290 spindles and finally, in the bottom spinning room, the weft mules of 1278 spindles. The other machinery would have been installed in the card room, extending into the extension at the back of the mill.

The steam engine of 1200 hp (0·89MW) was supplied by John Musgrave & Sons Limited of Bolton and described in some detail by the *Stockport Advertiser*.[60] The engine was in fact a pair of engines, these being horizontal tandem compound engines, each having a 25 inch diameter high pressure and a 44 inch diameter low pressure cylinder. They were fitted with Corliss valves to the high pressure cylinders, regulated by Musgrave's Patent cut-off motion. The low pressure cylinders had double posted slide valves. The frames were of box section, with the slide bars, which were double bars, cast upon them. The crank pedestals were secured to the frames by wrought iron bolts and were fitted with steps of phosphor bronze arranged in four ports and made adjustable by means of solid wedges and screws. The crank shaft was of Sir Joseph Whitworth's fluid compression steel having necks 16 inch diameter by 3 feet long and increasing to 22 inch diameter on the wheel bore. Cranks, cross-heads and connecting rods were of hammered scrap iron, machined and polished. The crank pins were also of Sir Joseph Whitworth's fluid compressed steel having a diameter of 10 inches. The 7 inch diameter cross shafts and 6 inch diameter piston rods were also of steel. The pistons were of cast-iron with Buckley's patent packing. The air-pumps were of 30 inch diameter, a stroke of 2 feet, and were driven off the cross-shafts by wrought iron levers. The engines ran at 50 rpm with a stroke of 5 feet. The flywheel which weighed over 70 tons had a diameter of 32 feet and it carried 32 1⅝ inch cotton drive ropes. The rim was built up of 12 segments, supported by 24 arms secured to two centre bosses. The barring engine was Musgrave's patent with automatic releasing mechanism and geared into a spun ring cast into the inside rim of the flywheel.

The boilers, to Stott & Sons specification, were supplied by Thomas Oldham of Wellington Boiler Works, Heaton Norris, Stockport. They were also described in some detail by the *Stockport Advertiser* but were fairly standard Lancashire boilers. There were four of them of Dalzeil steel, producing steam at 100psi, 7 feet 6 inches in diameter and 30 feet long with two 3 feet diameter flues. The shells were of half inch plates in 10 rings of two plates each butt jointed in longitudinal seams. The flues were of 7/16 inch plates, also in ten rings welded longitudinally and connected with flanged joints. Each flue had five conical pipes, welded in cross positions. The ends were of 9/16 inch plates, in one piece, stayed with 5 gusset stays above the flues and two below, also with two longitudinal stays. The front end was turned up along with the angle iron ring while the back end was flanged with the flue holes bored out. All the edges of the plates were planed, all rivet holes drilled after the plates were bent into position and the riveting done by machinery.

How the machinery installed in the Old Mill was driven is not clear. To drive it from the No.1 Mill engine would have required a very long line shaft running through the whole length of the No.1 Mill into the Old Mill. Alternatively the Old Mill may have had its own, existing, engine, which would have been supplied with steam from the boiler house on the river bank. If there was such an engine it would have been installed in an engine house internal to the mill and would probably have been a beam engine, but there is no evidence of this on the architect's perspective view (fig.15).

60 'Palmer Mills Engines', *Stockport Advertiser*, 1/7/1887, 8d. Note the other article 'Palmer Mills Company, Engines Started by the Mayor', *Stockport Advertiser*, 1/7/1887, 7c-d, states the engine to be of 1100hp. Quoted engine powers could vary by this amount according to whether they are design or indicated powers; the figure of 1200hp is stated to be indicated horse power.

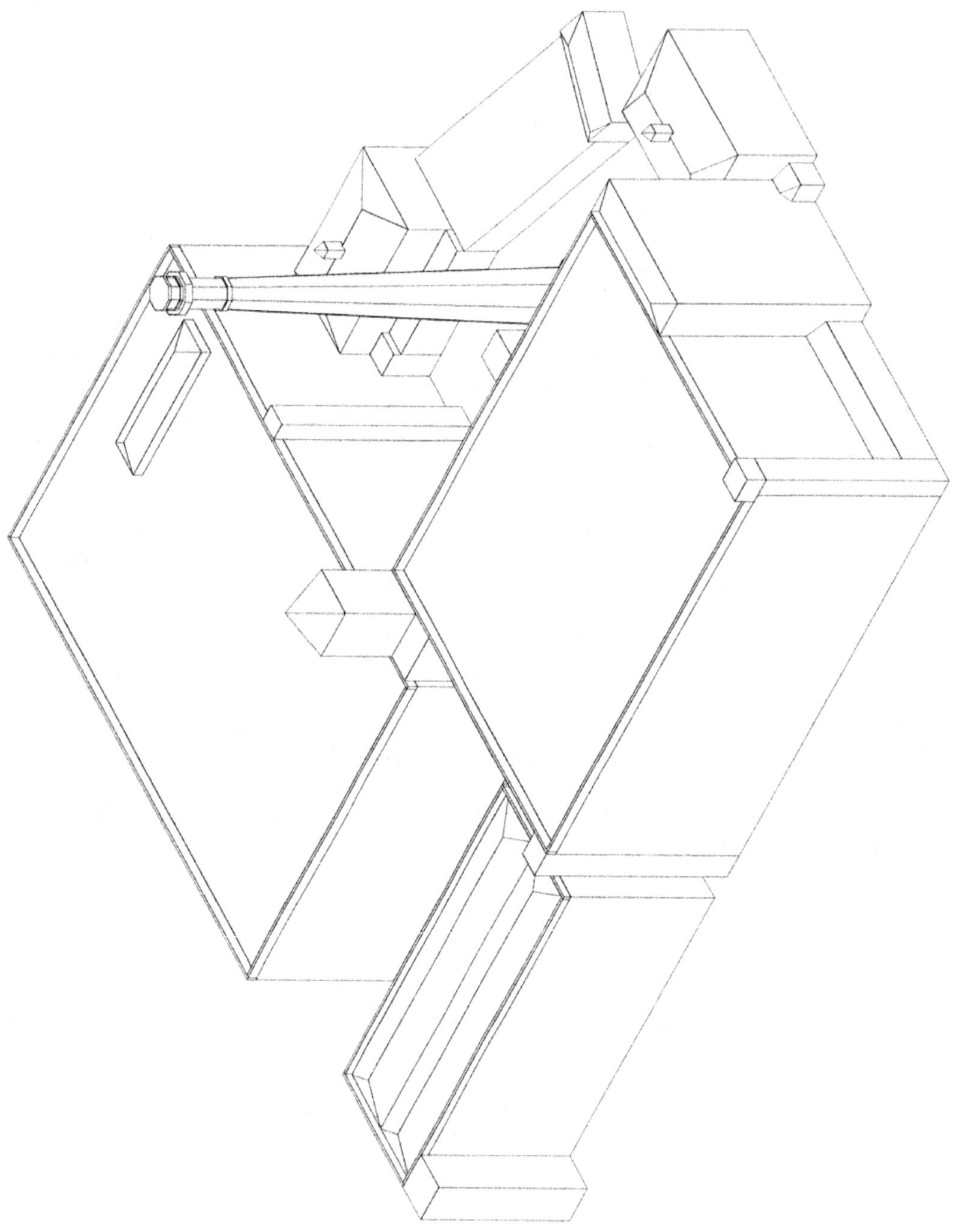

Fig.24 Isometric view of Palmer Mills from the north-west. This view includes the dust flue of 1915 attached to the north-east corner of the Old Mill.

Fig.25 Aerial view from the north-west taken sometime between 1931, when the waterless gas holder was built, and 1937, when Palmer No.1 Mill was demolished. The main subject of interest is clearly the gas works, but the Palmer Mills can be seen just above the gas holders with the Vernon Mills beyond.

See acknowledgements (p.vii).

Fig.26 Aerial view from the north-west, also taken some time between 1931 and 1937. The main object of this view is again the Gas Works but Palmer Mills can be seen to the left, complete with both No.1 and No.2 Mills and the Old Mill fronting Mersey Street. Prominent on the front of the Old Mill is the enlarged dust flue built in 1915. To the left is Vernon No.2 Mill.

See acknowledgements (p.vii).

Fig.27 1920's aerial view from south. Again a view of the Gas Works, but most of Palmer Mills are visible to the right. This view must pre-date 1931 because the waterless gas holder has not yet been built. Vernon Park Primary School in the foreground.

Stockport Local Heritage Library.

Fig.28 View of Palmer Mills from the south-west in 1915. In the left foreground the No.1 Mill and engine house, No.2 Mill in the right background. The ornamental top on the hoist of No.1 Mill which so annoyed Matthew Travis can be seen behind the chimney. By contrast the top of the hoist on No.2 Mill is plain. In this view the water tower is hidden by the chimney.

'Interesting Installation of Opening Machinery', *Textile Recorder*, (33: 389), 15/8/1915, 102 (fig.3).

Fig.29 A more distant view from the south-west of unknown date. Vernon Mills can be seen to the right. Vernon Park School is in the foreground.

Stockport Local Heritage Library.

Fig.30 Palmer No.2 Mill from the south. Meadow Mill of J. & T. Leigh in left background. Vernon No.1 Mill to the right, the space between it and Palmer No.2 Mill was originally occupied by Vernon No.2 Mill. (12/01/1992)

Fig.31 Palmer No.2 Mill (left) with Vernon No.1 Mill (right) viewed from the south-west. Vernon Park School in the foreground. (15/02/1987)

7. CONSTRUCTION OF THE No.2 MILL

Despite statements at the end of 1887 that its was hoped to rapidly proceed to No.2 Mill it was some time before any action was taken, it being reported in mid-October 1888 that the architects, Stott & Sons, were surveying the site and preparing the plans.[61] When this was announced at the next quarterly meeting of the company on Friday, 2 November 1888, one of the shareholders, Matthew Travis, asked if they were going to spend money on an 'architects mill'.[62] He continued: 'Anybody who had been on the top of the present mill would have seen that it was about six feet higher than it ought to be in one part. There was a lot of work behind the chimney which was not seen and he had heard complaints about hundreds of pounds being spent needlessly. No doubt the architect had been showing off a bit, but they had a voice in the matter as well'. The Chairman in reply said that Travis was referring to the ornamental top on the hoist (fig.28), they would not put one on the new hoist and would not have agreed to the present one if they had known what the result would be, but things look different on paper to what they do in fact. But the new mill, he continued, would have some uniformity with the first but the cost would be kept down as much as possible.

In January 1889 it was reported that work on No.2 Mill was proceeding with the contract for the foundations having been let to Jonathan Partington of Chadderton.[63] It is evident that the whole building contract in fact went to Jonathan Partington, instead of T. & W. Meadows who had built the No.1 Mill. The iron beams were to be supplied by Dunkerley and Company of Manchester. Dunkerley's were iron merchants, not producers, and, although described as iron, the beams were in fact of steel, rolled by the Leeds Steel Works. The machinery was again to be ordered from Asa Lees of Oldham, although was not entered into their order books until 3 May 1889. In March it was reported that the order for boilers had again been placed with T. Oldham of Wellington Boiler Works, Heaton Norris, Stockport.[64]

As with No.1 Mill, construction of No.2 Mill was marred by a fatal accident. This occurred on Monday, 18 March 1889, when demolishing part of the old mills. This resulted in the deaths of two man, John Cronan and Patrick McCormack, and serious injury of three others, named Trench, Boyle and Deaville. The inquest returned a verdict of 'accidental death', saying that there was no fault on the part of the Foreman Howard. Nevertheless, the three injured and the relatives of the deceased subsequently sued the contractor, Jonathan Partington for damages, the case being heard at Stockport County Court on Friday, 13 December 1889. The amount claimed was £218 each and it was claimed that the two foremen were partially drunk that day and had been quarrelling with each other. Damages were awarded but not to the amount claimed. Of the injured, Trench was awarded £100, Boyle £75 and Deaville £25. The wife of the deceased Patrick McCormack received £140 while the mother of John Cronan received £100. While no more fatal accidents are reported, three more men working on No.2 Mill were injured on Thursday, 8 August 1889 when a scaffold collapsed.[65] Under modern health and safety legislation these accidents would undoubtedly have led to prosecutions.

The capital of the company appears to have been split informally into accounts for the two mills. At the quarterly meeting in August 1889 the chairman remarked that people preferred to buy shares in the No.1 Mill rather than No.2 Mill, however some 5000 shares in No.2 Mill had been taken up. This division of capital is not reflected in the returns to the Companies Registrar which simply report that 15 399 shares had been issued by 20 February 1890. It was stated at the August 1889 meeting that No.2 Mill should be roofed in by the end of October and ready to start in the New Year. However, this target seems not to have been met and the reports of the next two quarterly meetings in October and February make no mention of progress on the No.2 Mill. At the February 1890 meeting Councillor White had a matter which he said gave him great pain to mention, that under the shadow of their mill there was a public house which had 'come into hands nearly related to their manager and he believed the spinning master also'. The chairman replied

---

61 'The New Palmer Mill', *Stockport Advertiser*, 19/10/1888, 12d.

62 'Palmer Mills Company', *Stockport Advertiser*, 9/11/1888, 9d.

63 'Palmer Mills Company', *Stockport Advertiser*, 11/1/1889, 9e. This actually gives Jonathan Partington's address as 'Chatterton', this is clearly a misprint for Chadderton, although his address was more commonly given as Middleton Junction.

64 'Palmer Mill Boilers', *Stockport Advertiser*, 22/3/1889, 8f.

65 'Catastrophe at Palmer Mills-Inquest', *Stockport Advertiser*, 22/3/1889, 7f-g. 'The Palmer Mills Disaster - The Adjourned Inquest', *Stockport Advertiser*, 29/3/1889, 7g. 'Scaffold Accident at Palmer Mills', *Stockport Advertiser*, 9/8/1889, 8d. 'A Stockport Mill Disaster - Heavy Claims Against the Contractor', *Stockport Advertiser*, 20/12/1889, 10d.

that he did not think that this was a matter for discussion at a public meeting while another shareholder thought there was no need to fear collusion. This would have been the 'Coach and Horses' on the corner of Mersey Street and Queen Street, visible on the aerial photographs directly facing the No.2 Mill (fig.1 & 78); it was demolished in 1999.[66]

Not until the August 1890 was the chairman able to report that No.2 Mill was just beginning to spin and not until May 1891 was it reported to be all at work, with the No.2 engine proving to be more economical than the No.1 engine. However, at the August 1890 meeting, Councillor White had another awkward question to raise. This concerned rumours that in filling vacancies they tended to employ people other than Stockport people, certainly there seemed to be a large number of strangers in the self-actor department. This of course echoed concerns raised earlier by the trades union. The chairman replied blandly that the instructions to the manager and foreman were to employ the best people and it was hoped they would not have to go outside Stockport for them.[67] The *Oldham Chronicle* took on a more moralising tone:

> It is evident from the remarks of one of the shareholders at the meeting of the Palmer Mills Company that Stockport work people were not considered by the manager of that concern to be quite as competent as those hailing from outside the town. A good deal of the success of a company depends upon this point and there is no doubt that the superiority and adaptability of the work people is a leading factor in the supremacy of Oldham as a cotton spinning centre. The finest mill and the best machinery are of little avail unless superintended by the best manual skill. In the case of Palmer Mill, therefore, it is only likely that the manager will engage the most skilful hands he can get, and if Stockport folks do not answer to this description the fault is theirs and not his. A limited spinning company is not a charitable concern.[68]

The writer conveniently forgets that the less dynamic cotton industry of Stockport afforded fewer opportunities for people to acquire the skills. In Oldham when starting a new mill there was always a ready supply of big piecers in existing mills who were ready to move to becoming mule minders and could thus be recruited for the new mill. In Stockport there would not have been such a ready supply of big piecers. Similarly for card room staff.

There may have been a ceremonial starting of the engines, but no report can be located.[69] It had taken some 18 months from the start of construction to commencing production and another nine months before the mill was fully at work. Again this was rather slow by Oldham standards.

There are no contemporary figures for the original construction costs but the company balance sheet for 18 February 1909,[70] under 'Assets' details the following figures:

Buildings	£96 602	12s	6d
Machinery	£90 007	8s	3d
Total	£186 610	0s	9d

These figures will cover both mills and there is no statement that they are 'at cost' but as depreciation follows as a separate item the implication is that they are. But they will also include a certain amount of machinery purchased later, including ring spindles (see below). With these qualifications, this figure suggests a cost of approximately £1 2s (£1·10) per spindle. This exceeds by 7s (£0·35), or 47%, the original hope of building a mill for 15s (£0·75) per spindle. If 15s per spindle was considered to be 4s or 5s less than an Oldham mill then in fact they had exceeded the cost of building a mill in Oldham.

---

66 'The Palmer Mills Company - Quarterly Meeting of Shareholders', *Stockport Advertiser*, 9/8/1889, 10f. 'Palmer Mills Dividend', *Stockport Advertiser*, 11/10/1889, 8d. 'Palmer Mills Meeting', *Stockport Advertiser*, 14/2/1890, 10f.

67 'Palmer Mills Co.Ltd. - Employment of "foreigners"', *Stockport Advertiser*, 15/8/1890, 8f. 'Palmer Mills' *Stockport Advertiser*, 8/5/1891, 5b.

68 'Commercial Notes', *Oldham Chronicle*, 23/8/1890, 8g.

69 Unfortunately, there are quite a number of missing pages in the micro-film copies of the *Stockport Advertiser* held by the Stockport Local Heritage Library around this time so there may have been a report on one of the missing pages.

70 Filed in PRO BT31/14779/20252. This is the earliest available balance sheet.

N
No.1 Mill
STAIR TOWER
Hoist
21'
21'
ENGINE HOUSE
ROPE RACE
Centre lines of columns
PALMER No.2 MILL, STOCKPORT
GROUND PLAN
This is a sketch only, not accurate in all details and not to scale.
Derived from site survey.

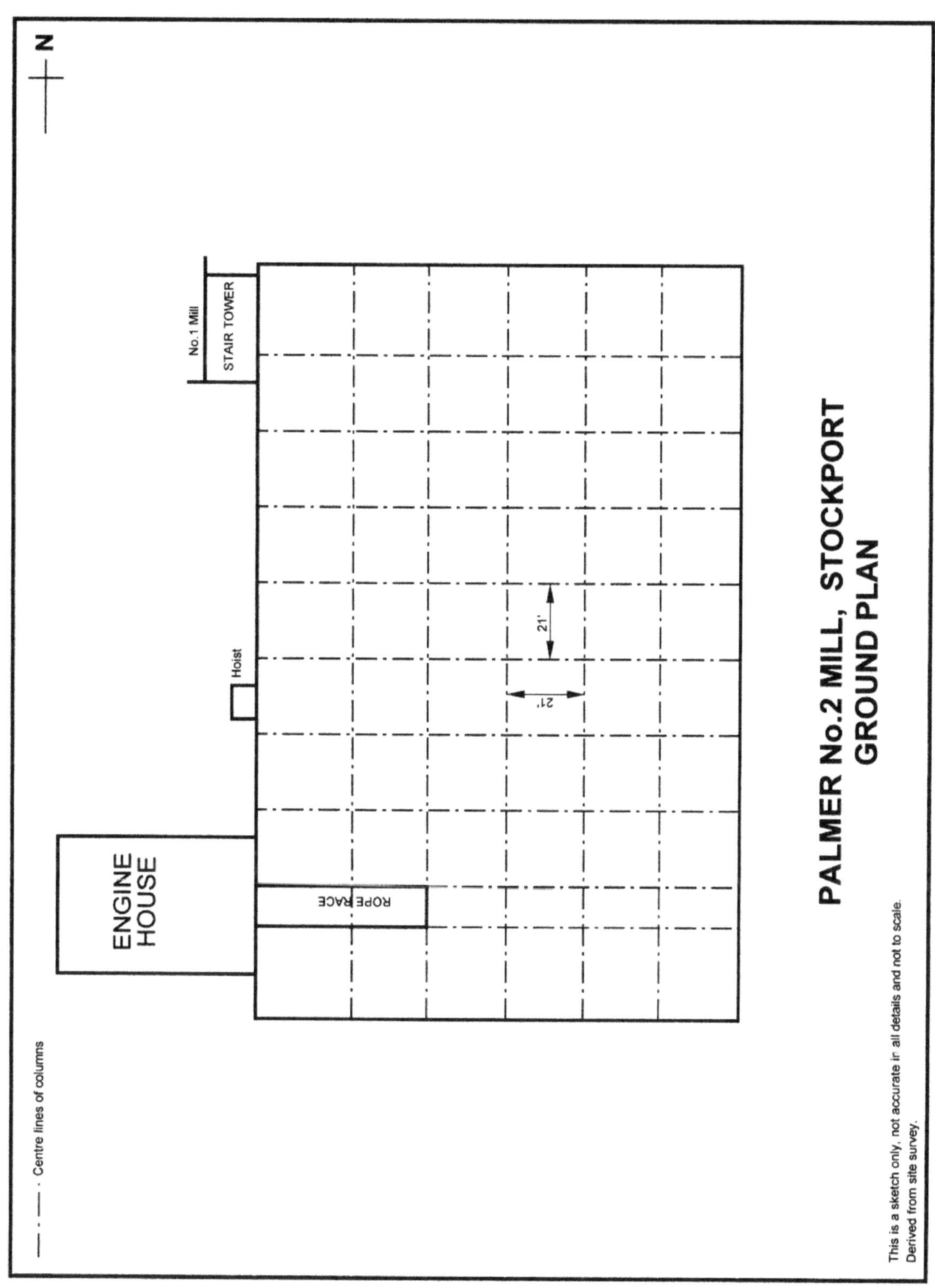

Fig.32

4th Spinning Room
3rd Spinning Room
2nd Spinning Room
1st Spinning Room
Card Room
Cellar
PALMER No.2 MILL, STOCKPORT
CROSS SECTION
This is a sketch only, not accurate in all details and not to scale.
Derived from site survey. Floor heights not known.

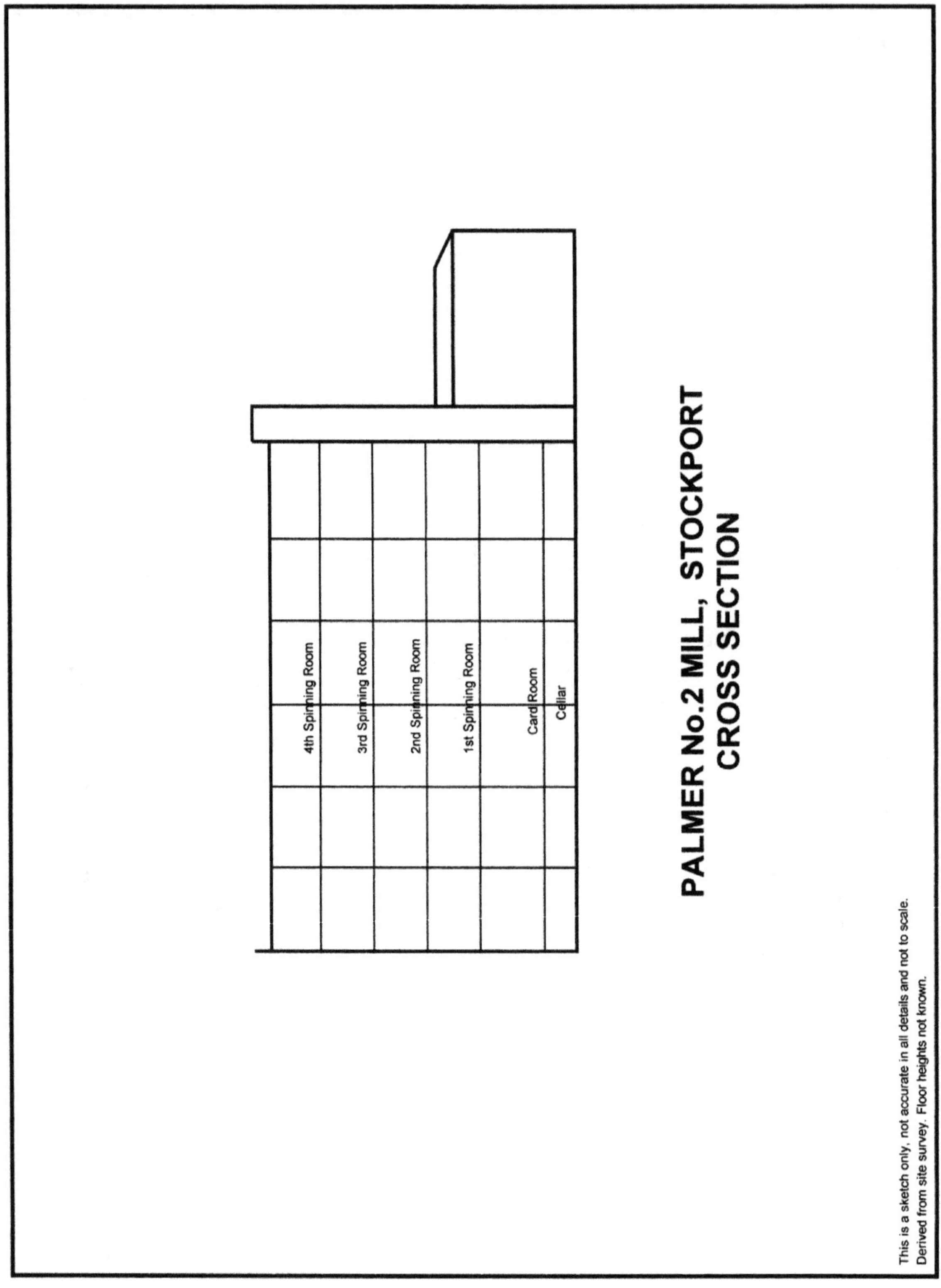

Fig.33

PALMER No.2 MILL, STOCKPORT
GIRDER PLAN
ROPE RACE
Main Girders
Secondary Girders
Columns
Brick Arches
Half Arches

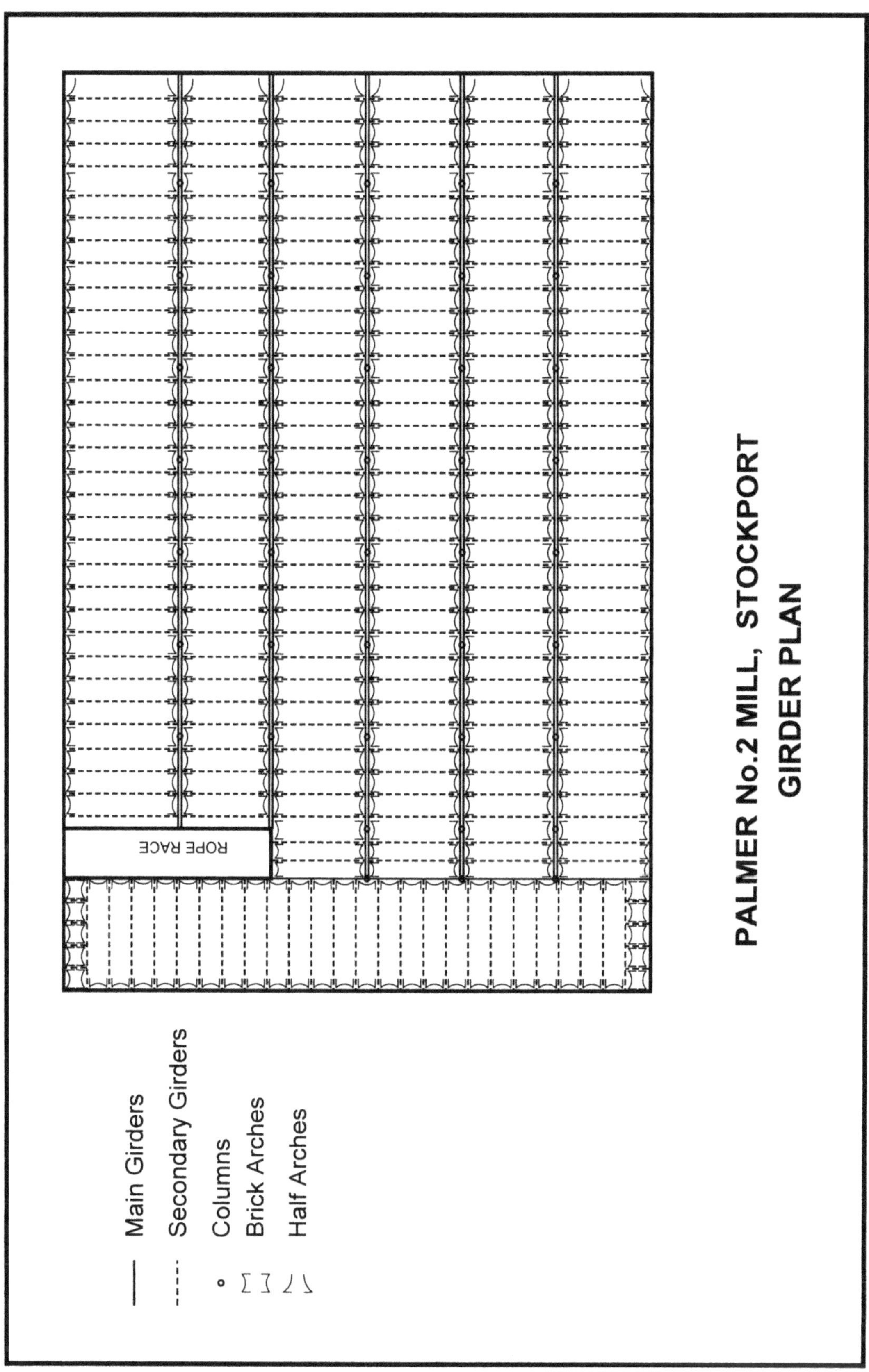

Fig.34

PALMER No.2 MILL, STOCKPORT
MULE ROOM LAYOUT
STAIR TOWER
Centre lines of columns
Gangway
Hoist
ROPE RACE
Pair of mules
3rd Spinning Room
4th Spinning Room
ROPE RACE

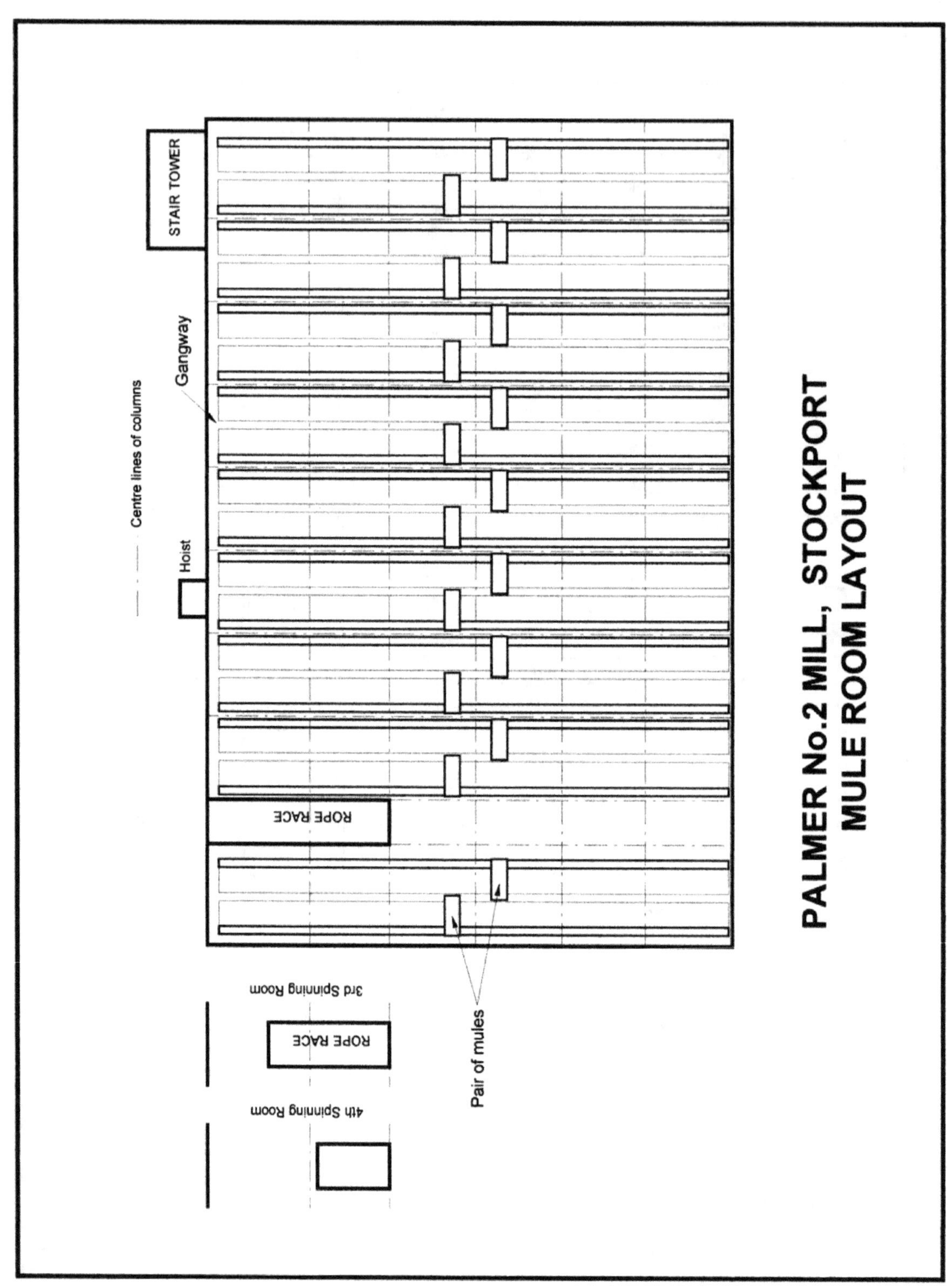

Fig.35

8. DESCRIPTION OF THE No.2 MILL

The No.2 Mill occupied the south-east corner of the site, previously occupied by buildings A & B (fig.7 & 14), building C to the north was retained in part or whole. The main axis of No.2 Mill was at right-angles to the No.1 Mill and its north-west corner abutted the staircase tower of No.1 Mill which now served both mills. It was the same height as the No.1 Mill with six storeys, including cellar, and approximately the same width of about 130 feet (39·6m). However, at nine bays it was one bay longer than the No.1 Mill with a length of about 200 feet (61m).

The south wall of the mill stood directly on the river bank and extended down to below basement level so there were windows into the basement on this south side (fig.46). The wall at basement level was thicker than the walls above with buttresses extending up from it to first floor level. Similar buttresses appeared on the east wall of the mill.

The remaining part of the old mills stood to the north of No.2 Mill and was connected to it at ground, that is card room, level by a single storey connecting block, which was probably built as part of the No.2 Mill. There is no direct photographic or documentary evidence for the form of this connecting block but it evidently existed because the whole of this area is shown by the large scale Ordnance Survey plans as being covered. The north wall of No.2 Mill as it latterly stood showed that it can only have been connected to the Old Mill at ground floor level (fig.39). This must have acted as the card room extension for the No.2 Mill.

The layout of No.2 Mill was the same as No.1 Mill with the cellar used for conditioning and warehousing, the card room occupying the ground floor with four mule spinning rooms above (fig.33). The Old Mill continued to act as the opening room for both mills.

The layout of the engine house and rope race of the No.2 Mill was somewhat awkward. In order to maximise the use of space the end wall of the mill was directly on the river bank, making it impossible to locate the rope race with the engine house centred on it on this wall. So there is one bay then the rope race (see fig.32). The boiler house adjoined the engine house and was a combined boiler house for both mills, using the existing chimney. The engine house was basically the same in design as that for No.1 Mill, being a lofty structure rising to the height of the first spinning room (fig.28, 33, & 45). It was rectangular in plan with tall arched windows, five along the long side and two in the short side. The hipped roof originally had a prominent ventilator in the centre but this had been removed by the time the mill was demolished. It was surrounded with a dentilated cornice but lacked the decorative corner parapets of the No.1 Mill engine house.

The yarn hoist projected in the centre of the west wall of the mill and, in deference to the wishes of the shareholders, it was flush with the roof without the decorative top to the hoist of No.1 Mill (fig.28).[71] The corners of the mill were, however, decorated in the same way as No.1 Mill with recessed panelling and open work parapets (fig.47); hopefully the shareholders found this acceptable. The windows to the top floor had stone key stones and stonework at the springing of the window arches, with panelling in the brickwork between the windows.

The walls were built on a stone plinth (fig.40) and were of red brick laid in English Garden Wall bond, which was the normal bond for mills of this period. The window sills were of stone which on the first and tops floors was extended to form a continuous stone band around the mill. The arch headed windows were divided into nine lights, three by three, and in some windows the middle or the top centre pane could be opened (fig.41).

The internal structure of the No.2 Mill was the same as the No.1 Mill, following Stott & Sons 1885 patent fireproof construction, giving them an identical appearance (fig.49). The girder plan (fig.34) shows how the arches were turned through 90 degrees at the south end of the mill, but not at the north end where they terminated with half-arches abutting the wall, with corbelled brick supports on alternate piers. When the mill was demolished it was found that there were columns embedded in the wall here rather than the girder ends being supported by the brick wall pier. This is unusual and it is suggested that this was done so

[71] The hipped roof which latterly topped the hoist tower was a later addition.

that at some future date the Old Mill to the north could be demolished and the No.2 Mill readily extended into its place.

The roof was a flat, tank, roof, interrupted by the roof light for the rope race at its south-west corner (fig.1). Flat roofs needed overflows and this is the purpose of the down pipes on the south wall (fig.46).

The cast iron columns diminished in diameter progressing up the mill, the largest being in the basement where they had to support the much heavier card room machinery as well as the rest of the mill above. The columns were mounted in the basement on stone bases. The card room floor consisted of stone flags which were still in place when the mill was demolished as were the wooden boards which covered the floors above. The main and secondary girders were of steel, the structure of the No.2 Mill being in advance of the No.1 Mill in this respect. Although, as noted above, it was reported that the 'iron beams were to be supplied by Dunkerley and Co. of Manchester', when the mill was demolished the main girders were found to be stamped 'Leeds Steel Company', showing that they were in fact of steel (fig.65, 66 & 73).[72]

The entrances from the staircase onto each floor had moulded door cases, that on the top floor being more elaborate than the rest (fig.64).

There was a water tower for the fire sprinkler system above the staircase. It is not clear when this was built. It appears in the architect's perspective view of the No.1 Mill (fig.15) but the date of this view is not known. The drawings for No.1 Mill simply label it as staircase and 1885 would be a very early date for a sprinkler system to be installed. The adjacent Vernon Mills of 1881 and 1884 were not built with sprinkler systems. It is possible that it was added at the time of construction of the No.2 Mill as by this date mills were beginning to be equipped with sprinkler systems. The water tower was of brick with light coloured stone bands, small windows grouped in threes, a stone dentilated cornice and surmounted originally by a pyramid roof.

The 1930s aerial photograph shows a fire escape on the north front of the No.1 Mill (fig.25). This was probably a later addition because it is not shown on the architect's perspective. As the No.2 Mill latterly stood, there was an external cast-iron fire escape on the east side of the mill (fig.37 & 38), but none on any of the other sides. A serious fire at the adjacent Vernon No.1 Mill in 1902 resulted in the deaths of a number of persons, one of the factors being a lack of external fire-escapes.[73]

[72] This disproves the suggestion made in Holden, *Stott & Sons*, 68, that Stott & Sons moved to steel girders when they introduced the triple-brick arch system.

[73] 'Disastrous Mill Fire at Stockport', *Textile Mercury,* 8/11/1902, 358. http://historyservices.webeden.co.uk/#/isaac-peet-vernon-mill-fire/4591939865 (accessed 17/02/2017).

Fig.36 No.2 Mill from the north-west. Showing the water tower and the blank wall where it was originally joined to the No.1 Mill. The projection with windows on the west side is the original hoist tower, the windowless projection between it and the water tower is a later addition. (06/12/1998)

Fig.37 No.2 Mill from the north-east, with the 'To Let' notices attached to the roof which were a prominent feature of the mill in the mid-1980s. Note the fire escape on the outside of the east wall. In the foreground is the site of Vernon No.2 Mill, now being taken for the new road (St. Mary's Way) and a motor show room. (23/03/1986)

Fig.38 A later view of No.2 Mill from the north-east after completion of St. Mary's Way. This shows the eastern office block built after demolition of the Old Mill in the 1930's. (12/01/1992)

Fig.39 Detail of the north side of No.2 Mill showing where the ground floor was connected to the Old Mill. (06/12/1998)

Fig.40 Detail of the east side of No.2 Mill showing the stone plinth on which the mill was built. (06/12/1998)

Fig.41 No.2 Mill. Detail of the first and second floor windows on the east side. (12/01/1992)

Fig.42 No.2 Mill from the south-east showing the original footbridge, known as Captain's Bridge, linking New Bridge Lane and Queen Street. On the right is the remaining part of Vernon No.2 Mill. Note in the background the waterless gas holder which was demolished in 1988. (07/05/1983)

Fig.43 A later view of No.2 Mill from the south east after St. Mary's Way had been completed, with a new road bridge replacing the footbridge. The remaining part of Vernon No.2 Mill and the water-less gas holder have also been demolished. (12/01/1992)

Fig.44 No.2 Mill from the south-west. (12/01/1992)

Fig.45 No.2 Mill Engine House. View from the south. The rectangular windows were later additions. (12/01/1992)

Fig.46 Detail of south wall of No.2 Mill with the engine house to the left. This side of the mill fronted onto the river bank, the river itself being out of sight at the bottom of the picture. The bottom windows here are in the basement. Note the buttressing of the wall up to the first floor level and the drain pipes. (12/01/1992)

Fig.47 No.2 Mill. Detail of south-east corner. (12/01/1992)

Fig.48 View from the west with Palmer No.2 Mill in the centre. Beyond it is Vernon No.1 Mill. The chimney to the right is that of Pear Mill, to the left Ark (Welkin) Ring Mill. The waterless gas holder that previously obstructed this view of Palmer No.2 Mill was demolished in 1988. (15/04/1991)

Fig.49 View of the ground floor of No.2 Mill showing the quadruple brick-arch, Stott & Son's Patent, construction. (19/08/1995)

9. EQUIPMENT OF THE No.2 MILL

There is no record of the blowing room and opening equipment, but presumably this was again ordered from Lord Brothers of Todmorden and installed in the Old Mill. The rest of the machinery was ordered from Asa Lees and entered in their order books on 3 May 1889 although subsequently, on the 14 February 1890, a number of alterations were made to the orders which are marked in red ink. With the exception of draw frames, the order books for which do not survive, the card room machinery as finally delivered was:

66	double, roller and clearer, carding engines.		
??	draw frames.		
9	slubbing frames of 96 spindles.	864	spindles in total.
18	intermediate frames.	2588	spindles in total.
	consisting of		
	16 of 144 spindles.	2304	spindles in total.
	2 of 142 spindles.	284	spindles in total.
45	roving frames of 176 spindles.	7920	spindles in total.

This was a very late date to be ordering roller and clearer cards rather than the superior revolving flat cards, but possibly that had decided to keep the machinery the same as in the No.1 Mill.

The original order for mules was straight forward, 72 mules with a total of 88 776 spindles, clearly spilt into groups of 18, that is nine pairs per floor:[74]

54	1⅛ inch gauge weft mules,	69 552 spindles in total.	
	consisting of:		
	18 of 1278 spindles.	23 004 spindles in total.	Length 125ft.
	18 of 1290 spindles.	23 220 spindles in total.	Length 126ft.
	18 of 1296 spindles.	23 328 spindles in total.	Length 126ft 6in.
18	1⅜ inch spindle gauge twist mules of 1068 spindles.	19 224 spindles in total.	Length 127ft.

These are the same lengths as in No.1 Mill, except that No.1 Mill had two twist mules of only 1062 spindles. Perhaps with plans for the new mill having been finalised they realised they could squeeze in a extra 180 spindles and on 14 February 1890 the order was altered to 72 mules with a total of 88 956 spindles:

54	1⅛ inch gauge weft mules,	69 672 spindles in total.	
	consisting of:		
	4 of 1278 spindles.	5 112 spindles in total.	Length 125ft.
	18 of 1284 spindles.	23 112 spindles in total.	Length 125ft 6in.
	18 of 1290 spindles.	23 220 spindles in total.	Length 126ft.
	14 of 1302 spindles.	18 228 spindles in total.	Length 127ft.
18	1⅜ inch spindle gauge twist mules	19 284 spindles in total.	
	consisting of:		
	4 of 1062 spindles.	4 248 spindles in total.	Length 126ft 6in.
	14 of 1074 spindles.	15 036 spindles in total.	Length 128ft.

The original order fitted very logically into the mill with 18 mules on each floor but it is difficult to see immediately how the revised order was arranged in the mill. Each floor must have had two pairs of shorter mules, thus:

[74] Lengths are given to the nearest 6in, allowing 5ft for the headstock and frame ends, the exact figure not being known for Asa Lees mules.

Spinning Room 1:
4 weft mules of 1278 spindles,
14 weft mules of 1284 spindles.
Spinning Room 2:
4 weft mules of 1284 spindles,
14 weft mules of 1290 spindles.
Spinning Room 3:
4 weft mules of 1290 spindles,
14 weft mules of 1302 spindles.
Spinning Room 4:
4 twist mules of 1062 spindles,
14 twist mules of 1074 spindles.

The shorter mules on each floor may have been installed in the bays either side of the rope race because of difficulties of access in this area. Alternatively they may have been installed in the two bays to the north end of the mill adjoining the staircase. It will be noted that in No.1 Mill the entrance from the stairs was directly in line with the gangway where as in No.2 Mill a turn of 90 degrees out of the staircase was required (fig.23 & 35). Shorter mules here would have allowed for greater landing area and ease of access.

In total the two mills had 136 mules with 167 400 spindles made up of:

100 weft mules, 128 904 spindles,
36 twist mules, 38 496 spindles.

This gives a ratio of 77% weft to 23% twist spindles.

Unfortunately, we know less about the engine and boilers of No.2 Mill than those of No.1 Mill. The engine was also supplied by John Musgrave of Bolton and has been recorded as a twin tandem compound developing 1700ihp (1·27MW) at 53rpm with two 22 inch high, two 46 inch low pressure cylinders and 60 inch stroke.[75] No.2 Mill was larger than No.1 Mill, with more spindles and hence more preparative machinery, so needed a larger engine. Also, as noted above, it was stated to be of a different design which was proving more economical. Again we have no detailed information as to the boilers apart from the fact that they were also supplied by T.Oldham and another four would undoubtedly have been needed.

---

[75] Mill Engines Database, Northern Mill Engines Society (NMES), information extracted by Richard Hills from records held by Courtaulds Technical Department in the 1960s (personal communication from John Phillp 7/01/2000).

10. OPERATION OF THE MILLS TO 1919

The yarn counts advertised by the mill in the 1892 edition of Worrall's *Directory* were 30-36 twist and 36-54 weft. By 1900 this range of counts had been narrowed to 32-36 twist and 36-48 weft and by 1908 the weft range had narrowed again to 36-46.[76] This classified the mill as a medium to fine counts mill, fine is so far as it produced weft counts above 40. American cotton was spun so Palmer Mill could be classed as an Oldham counts mill.

After 1900 some additions to the machinery were made and some machinery was replaced. This machinery was purchased from Howard & Bullough of Accrington, rather than Asa Lees, the original suppliers. Most important was the addition of ring frames, eventually implementing a proposal included in the original company prospectus of 1884. By 1908 there were 2304 ring spindles, by 1913 this had increased to 9768 and 13 768 by 1921. This was still considerably less than the 35 000 suggested by the 1884 prospectus. In 1911 the mill was advertising ring spun twist yarn of counts 34 to 36. In absolute terms the mill now had a total of 181 168 spindles, or 188 052 in mule equivalent terms, where one ring spindle is considered to be equal to 1·5 mule spindles. In mule equivalent terms this gave the mill a total of 128 904 weft to 59 148 twist spindles, a ratio of 69% weft to 31% twist.

Although many records for Howard & Bullough survive as part of the Platt-Saco-Lowell archive at the Lancashire Archives, Preston, there is insufficient to trace these orders in detail. There are no order books, nor are there any individual machine order books. But some information can be found in the series of volumes under the title 'Weekly Totals and Value of Machinery Ordered'. These give for each week customer names and the number of each type of machine ordered. So, for example, only the number of ring frames is given, not the type or number of spindles. Also there are gaps in these volumes from August 1900 to July 1905 and from February 1914 to July 1917.[77]

The available Howard & Bullough records include the following ring frame orders for Palmer Mill:

15/07/1905 3 frames;
29/04/1911 10 frames;
16/09/1911 6 frames.

The maximum length of ring frame quoted by Howard & Bullough is 500 spindles.[78] Some frames must have been ordered before July 1905 to make up the initial 2304 ring spindles. The 16 frames purchased in 1911 would have included the additional 7464 spindles installed by 1913, a further eight to ten frames must have been purchased after February 1914 to make up the additional 4000 spindles installed by 1921. This suggests a total of about 30 ring frames.

Presumably these ring frames were installed on the upper floors of the Old Mill as had been originally suggested, the blowing room only taking up the lower floors. It is somewhat paradoxical that while old mills like the original Palmer Mills were not suitable for modern mules, they were able to accommodate the newer technology of ring spinning. Not knowing the exact details of the ring frames at Palmer, it is not possible to give actuals dimensions but in round figures ring frames required about 10 feet per 100 spindles, so around 50 feet for 500 spindles, depending on the actual spindle gauge. These would have fitted into the approximately 55 feet depth of the Old Mill.

Ring frames were not the only machinery supplied to the mill by Howard & Bullough over these years and the following orders are also recorded:

---

76 Note that it is unclear whether the counts given in Worrall's *Lancashire Textile Directory* were the range of counts that a mill could spin or whether it is the actual range of counts that was spun.

77 LRO DDPSL/2/8. See under 'Documentary Sources' for detailed references. It may be thought that the sequence of volumes LRO DDPSL/3/9 Types of Machine on Order and Delivered should provide information but it is found that the entries in these volumes run from 1905 to 1907 and then start again in 1930.

78 Howard & Bullough Ltd., *Combined Catalogue and Machinery Calculations* (Accrington: Howard & Bullough Ltd., 1914), 128-31.

23/09/1905	1	beaming machine
05/09/1908	20	carding engines
26/09/1908	1	carding engine
03/12/1910	6	speed frames
08/04/1911	24	draw frames
01/07/1911	1	winding frame
01/07/1911	3	beaming machines
15/07/1911	3	draw frames
15/07/1911	8	speed frames
16/09/1911	1	winding frame
16/09/1911	2	beaming machines
02/12/1911	1	winding frame
21/09/1912	6	carding engines
12/10/1912	1	draw frame
12/04/1913	1	draw frame

Some of this is the additional preparation machinery, consisting of carding engines, draw frames and speed frames, required for the extra ring frames. The winding frames would be to re-wind yarns from the ring bobbins to larger warper's bobbins. The beaming machines then wound the yarn from the warper's bobbins onto weaver's beams for despatch to the weaving mill. It became common to despatch ring spun yarn in this way as it reduced operations in the weaving mill and reduced transport costs which would otherwise have been incurred in transporting and returning heavy ring bobbins. Presumably this machinery was also installed in the Old Mill.

There can be little doubt that at some time the whole of the roller and clearer carding engines originally installed in the mill would have been replaced by revolving flat carding engines. Although comment was made in 1919 on the mules being the original machines and hence obsolete, nothing was said about carding engines. A mill still operating roller and clearer carding engines at this date would undoubtedly attracted comment. More than the 20 recorded above would have been needed for this replacement although fewer carding engines would have been needed than originally leaving room in the card rooms for the additional machinery required by the ring frames.

The opening and blowing room machinery was renewed in 1915 with machinery from Howard and Bullough. There is no information on this order in the surviving records but an illustrated report of this installation was published in the *Textile Recorder* (fig.8-9, 28 & 50).[79] The installation occupied three floors of the Old Mill. Four sets of machinery were installed, two to supply each mill. The top most room had hopper bale openers, the intermediate floor mixing bins and hopper feeders and the lowest floor the openers and scutchers. The bale openers had long feed lattices enabling them to be fed from eight bales at a time and they delivered material down a chute onto feed lattices fixed in the ceiling of the floor below which directed the material to the mixing bins. The material from the mixing bins was fed into the hopper feeders which delivered it to conveying trunks and so to the openers installed on the floor below. The openers were Buckley openers which fed directly into the scutcher and lap machines. At the same time a new dust flue of larger dimensions was built on the north-east corner of the Old Mill indicating that the new machinery had higher processing capacity than the old.[80] This suggests that it had been intended to proceed to replace all the machinery in the mill in order to utilise this greater capacity. The use of stack mixings is surprising since Oldham mills had largely abandoned this practice by this date. Maybe the directors of Palmer Mills took a more conservative view or considered this to be the most suitable method for the qualities they were producing.

By 1901 only Johnson and Noden remained of the original directors. The full list of directors on 1 January 1901 was:

[79] 'Interesting Installation of Opening Machinery', *Textile Recorder*, (33: 389), 15/8/1915, 101-4.

[80] This can be identified on the Ordnance Survey plans of 1922 and 1934 and also on the 1930s aerial photographs (fig.25 & 26). It is also shown on the isometric view (fig.24).

Name	Address	Occupation
John Goode Johnson	Brinnington House, Stockport.	Bleacher.
John Emery	57 Adswood Lane East, Stockport.	Cotton spinner.
John Noden	2 Adswood Lane East, Stockport.	Provision dealer.
Tom Cocker	Stanley House, Stockport.	Hat leather cutter.
James Moorhouse	'Thorncliffe', Higher Brinksway, Stockport.	Out of business.

By this date there were only six shareholders who can be identified as being from the working classes. These were three labourers, a porter, a roller coverer and a winder. One held ten shares, one six, three five and one only two shares.

By 13 July 1917, the last return of directors before the company was re-constituted, there had been further changes on the board of directors. Although three persons remained the same, addresses and occupations had changed:

Name	Address	Occupation
John Emery	41 Hill Top Avenue, Cheadle Hulme.	Yarn doubler.
Tom Cocker	Stanley House, Edgeley, Stockport.	Leather dresser.
James Moorhouse	'Edenhurst', Ansdell Road South, Lytham St.Anne's, Lancashire.	Gentleman.
James Emery	14 Kennerly Road, Stockport.	Yarn doubler.
Frank Stafford Johnson.	Brinnington, Stockport.	Yarn doubler.

James Moorhouse previously described as 'out of business' had now retired to Lytham St.Annes and considered himself a 'Gentleman'. This tendency for directors of cotton spinning companies formed in the last quarter of the nineteenth century to have retired to the coast – Fylde, Southport or North Wales – by the time of the First World War while still retaining their directorships is a common one. This may explain in part the willingness of directors to sell their mills in the 1919-1920 re-floating boom. John and James Emery were presumably related and were directors, along with W.Emery, of William Emery Limited, cotton spinners and doublers of Howard Street Mills, Stockport. Frank Stafford Johnson was the sole partner in F.S.Johnson, doublers of Park Mill, Stockport. Whether he was related to John Goode Johnson is not known but seems likely.[81]

The final return of capital and shares for the original company is dated 13 February 1919 and this shows that the nominal capital remained at the original value of £100 000 in 20 000 £5 shares. £3 had been called up on each share. This contrasts with other companies of similar age who had reorganised their capital in the 1900s. At this date there were 251 shareholders who were geographically more dispersed than the original 194, although the vast majority, 179 or 71%, still came from Stockport:

Place	No. of Persons	Place	No. of Persons
Stockport	179	Denton, Lancashire	1
Manchester	21	Great Harwood, Lancashire	1
Liverpool	8	Heywood, Lancashire	1
London	4	Huddersfield, Yorkshire	1
Sheffield	4	Knutsford, Cheshire	1
Southport, Lancashire	3	Leigh, Lancashire	1
Blackburn, Lancashire	2	Liscard, Cheshire	1
Macclesfield, Cheshire	2	Lytham, Lancashire	1
Oldham, Lancashire	2	New Brighton, Cheshire	1
Sale, Cheshire	2	Newport, Shropshire	1
Tenbury, Worcestershire	2	Nottingham	1
Ashton-under-Lyne, Lancashire	1	Sutton, Surrey	1
Barnoldswick, Yorkshire	1	Timperley, Cheshire	1
Blackpool, Lancashire	1	Warrington, Lancashire	1
Bolton, Lancashire	1	Whitefield, Lancashire	1
Buxton, Derbyshire	1	Wilmslow, Cheshire	1
Chapel-en-le-Frith, Derbyshire	1	**Total**	251

[81] Worrall's *Lancashire Textile Directory,* 1911. Skinner's *Cotton Trade Directory*, 1923.

How many of the original shareholders remained at this date has not been analysed, but apart from one person described as a 'cotton operative' the working classes have disappeared from the shareholders list. At the meeting to approve the sale of the mill (see below), the chairman, John Emery, claimed that one third of the shares were held by the directors and their families.

Of the architects, Abraham Henthorn Stott had disposed of his 50 shares by 20 February 1890, evidently to his son Abraham Henthorn Stott, junior, who then held 100 shares in place of the original 50. His elder brother, Jesse Ainsworth Stott still held 50 shares. By 21 February 1895 the two brothers had increased their shareholdings, Abraham to 200 and Jesse to 150. They still held these shares on 18 February 1904 but by 18 February 1909, Abraham had disposed of his shares. Jesse retained his shares until his death on the 13 February 1917 when they passed to his three surviving children, James Henthorn Stott, Mary Harley Stott and Harold Ainsworth Stott, as his executors.[82] They disposed of these shares on 18 March 1918.

There are no records surviving relating to the workforce but standard practice enables something to be said about the numbers and types of workers in the mill. Mules were worked in pairs by an operative spinner with two assistants, the big piecer and the little piecer [83] An operative was more often known as a self-actor minder or simply minder. Thus there were three people per pair of mules. The original 64 mules in the No.1 Mill formed 32 pairs, requiring 96 people. The other tasks in the mill would have required around the same number of people, giving a total of around 200. The 72 mules in the No.2 Mill would have required 108 people, so the mill in total would have required around 220 people, or 420 for both mills. Only a very rough estimate of the numbers required for the ring frames can be made because of the uncertainty of the actual number of frames installed in the mull and also because as the numbers of people used in ring spinning could vary quite considerably.[84] Assuming 30 frames in the mill and two sides per ring spinner, this suggests 30 ring spinners plus 10 doffers and gaiters, a total of 40. Allowing a further 40 for the other tasks in the mill gives 80 people in all. This suggests a maximum workforce in the mills of around 500 people. No doubt much of the workforce lived in the terraced houses near the mill in Portwood or to the south of the river, walking to and from work across Captain's Bridge.

The main inputs to the mill were raw cotton and coal, the main purpose of the weighing machine by the entrance (fig.7 & 14) was to weigh these as they came in. The mill did not have a direct rail connection nor access from a canal so these would have arrived by road. The Portwood Goods Station of the Cheshire Lines Committee Railway was only a just over a quarter of a mile (500m) to the north, with a cotton warehouse and coal yard. This line connected directly with Liverpool for the transport of raw cotton. Coal could also have come through here, although there were local supplies available from collieries at Bredbury. Some yarn may have been consumed locally by the doubling industry or weaving mills in Stockport, otherwise it could also have been sent out via the Portwood Goods Station to weaving mills elsewhere in Lancashire.

---

82 The return of Share Capital and Shares for 14 February 1918 incorrectly gives James Henthorn Stott as James Henry Stott.

83 Harold Catling, *The Spinning Mule* (Newton Abbot: David & Charles, 1970), 154. John Jewkes and E.M.Grey, *Wages and Labour in the Lancashire Cotton Spinning Industry* (Manchester: Manchester University Press, 1935), 8-11; despite its title this only covers the final spinning process and not the preparative processes.

84 Jewkes & Grey, *Wages and Labour,* 116-130.

Fig.50 New scutchers installed in the Old Mill in 1915.
'Interesting Installation of Opening Machinery', *Textile Recorder* (33: 389), 15/8/1915, 103 (fig.4).

Fig.51 William Hopwood lived at 6 Gordon Street, Shaw, the right-hand end house of Fern Terrace, built 1885. (24/02/2017)

Fig.52 (left) 41 Manchester Road, Shaw, the home of William Bridge. (29/12/2016)
Fig.53 (right) 68 Farrow Street, Shaw, the home of Herbert Hargreaves. (29/12/2016)

Fig.54 The large detached house is Struan House, Chamber Road, Shaw, the home of Harry Dixon. (24/02/2017)

11. PALMER MILLS (1919) LIMITED

In common with many other cotton spinning companies, particularly in the Oldham area, Palmer Mill was taken over by a new company in 1919, the Palmer Mills (1919) Ltd. This was done by a group of investors who purchased the whole of the share capital of the company, then put it into liquidation, the assets being purchased by a new company which had a much greater capitalization, on the assumption that the large profits experienced by the industry at the end of the First World War were going to continue.

The re-floating of Palmer Mill was arranged by a syndicate of three persons, William Hopwood, Harry Dixon and William Bridge, from Shaw, Oldham, who were instrumental in the re-floating of a number of other mills. At the beginning of August 1919 an offer was made to the old company of £242 693 12s plus £20 000 compensation to the directors for loss of office. Cotton in bale and in process, yarn and waste plus coal was to be taken and paid for at valuation. According the *Oldham Chronicle* the total price paid for Palmer Mill was £315 000.[85]

This resolution was put to the shareholders at what the *Oldham Chronicle* described as a 'lively meeting' on Wednesday afternoon, 6 August 1919 at the Stockport Unitarian Schools.[86] The *Oldham Chronicle* reported at some length on this meeting, amongst the general excitement of mill sales, the adjoining column being headed ‘Big Deals – Many Mill Sales Negotiated’. The chairman, John Emery, urged the shareholders to accept the offer, carefully explaining its advantages to them:

> At this price for each £5 share (£3 paid) the shareholders will receive upwards of £10 10s after payment of all expenses. The directors have entered into a provisional contract for sale on these terms subject to the same being ratified by the shareholders in general meeting. The principal reasons influencing the directors to recommend the sale are:-
>
> (a) The price yields more than double the amount obtained for shares in the open market.
>
> (b) The purchase money when re-invested should show a considerable permanent increase on the dividends which have been paid and the uncalled liability of £2 per share will be cancelled
>
> (c) Loss of production owing to shorter hours.
>
> (d) Increases of all working expenses and labour disturbance.
>
> (e) The purchasers will accept any part of the purchase money on loan at 5 per cent without deduction of tax.
>
> The directors and their families hold more than one-third of the company's shares and are wholly in favour of the sale being ratified.
>
> ...The Chairman explained that the average return for the past 30 years had enabled the shareholders to receive 9 to 10 per cent. The sale at the agreed price, in addition to cancelling £2 liability, gave them upwards of 2½ times their capital, which if invested in loan with the new company would give a steady return of 25 per cent per annum or if invested in 5 per cent Government War stock would yield 15 per cent. The mills were 30 or 31 years old and in the course of the next few years it would be necessary to renew the mules at a cost of £90,000 or £100,000.

The shareholders did not, however, accept the recommendation of their chairman without argument. John Bateman said that the price was a bargain as a new mill could not be built for less than £5 per spindle and they ought to be able to get an offer of £13 or £14 per share. Not surprisingly the compensation offered to the director's proved controversial. This was to be a controversial feature of later mill re-floatations, but Palmer was evidently the first time this compensation had been offered.[87] John Batemen pointed out that the compensation offered far exceeded the remuneration they were paid for a three year term of office while F.R.Robinson thought it looked like bribery. On the other hand, Mr.J.Barnshaw, who had worked at the mill

---

[85] ‘New Capital Basis – Full Return of Spinning Company Changes – Turnovers and Reconstructions’, *Oldham Chronicle, Textile Trade Supplement*, 31/12/1920; reprinted in *Cotton Spinning Companies Financial Review 1921* (Oldham: Oldham Chronicle, 1921).

[86] ‘Palmer Mills’, *Oldham Chronicle*, 9/8/1919, 11c.

[87] ‘Easily Gotten – The Question of Compensation to Directors’, *Oldham Chronicle*, 27/12/1919, 13. This article does not give the actual name of the mill in question apart from the fact that it was a Stockport mill, but it is clear from the details given that Palmer Mill is being referred to.

for 20 years, reiterated the chairman's point that the mules were obsolete and considered that the scheme was in the best interests of the shareholders. An attempt was made to adjourn the meeting for 14 days but this was ruled out of order by W.Johnston, the company's solicitor. So the motion was put to the vote which went against the motion by 34 votes to 14. The directors then demanded a poll which carried the motion. This suggests that the large shareholders were in favour and out voted the small shareholders who were against, something which is known to have occurred in the case of other mill re-floatations. However, a further meeting was needed to confirm the resolution, this could not be held on the same evening, causing John Bateman to remark 'Very well, it will only strengthen us in our efforts to overthrow this autocracy which has pushed things down our throats this afternoon'.

The meeting to confirm the resolution was held twelve days later on Monday, 18 August 1919 and chaired by F.R.Robinson.[88] In the meantime a delegation of shareholders, F.R.Robinson, Dr.Reyner and John Bateman, had met the directors and had come to an agreement regarding the compensation. While the whole of the £20 000 was still accepted, the directors were to take only £5000, £2350 was to be divided between three long-standing employees of the company and the remaining £12 650 was to be divided amongst the shareholders. Of the three employees, Mr.William Braddock, the secretary, was to receive £1500, Mr.Beswick, the manager who had not been there as long, £600 and 'a retired engineer' £250. Although there seems to have been general consent to these sums offered to employees there was some tough questioning of them by one shareholder Mr.Hammond. John Bateman still considered that the mill could have been sold at a better price, a view endorsed by R.Hutchinson who said that the price was ridiculous compared with prices being offered for mills within the last week. Nevertheless, the resolutions were carried with only Mr.Hammond voting against.

The total price paid for Palmer Mills of £315 000 works out at £1·74 per spindle. This compares with an average of £2·92 per spindle for 155 companies sold in 1919 and 1920 tabulated by the *Oldham Chronicle*.[89] The lowest price paid was £0·80 per spindle for Clough Mill while the highest was £8·84 paid for Orme Ring Mill. Prices did increase during the boom, but in general older mills sold for less, the highest prices being paid for mills built just before the war. On a straight price per spindle basis ring mills sold for more than mule mills, on a mule equivalent basis the price for Orme Ring reduces to £5·89 per spindle and the highest price paid for a mule mill was £7·70 per spindle for Howe Bridge Mills.[90] So shareholders Bateman and Hutchinson may have been correct in their perception that they could have got more for the mill if they had waited but being an old mill with obsolete equipment they could not have commanded the highest prices. Note that it was considered that the mules needed replacing, not that they should be replaced with ring frames.

The new company was not registered until 16 September 1919, the mill in the first instance being sold to William Hopwood and Harry Dixon for £242 693 12s 0d. They then sold it to the new company for £262 693 12s 0d, sharing the profit of £20 000 between them. The figure of £315 000 quoted by the *Oldham Chronicle* will include the £20 000 compensation money plus material in stock. The new company had a share capital of £150 000 in 30 000 £5 shares, the increase in capital from £100 000 to £150 000 being smaller than in other mill re-floatations. The share capital represented only half the cost of purchase and only £1 10s per share was called up totalling £45 000. The remainder was made up of loans and bank overdraft, the company registering a mortgage debenture of £150 000 on 29 October 1919.

The directors of the new company were:

Name	**Address**	**Occupation**
William Hopwood	6 Gordon Street, Shaw, Oldham.	Cotton spinner.
Harry Dixon	Struan House, Chamber Road, Shaw, Oldham	Cotton spinner.
William Bridge	41 Manchester Road, Shaw, Oldham.	Cotton mill manager.
Herbert Hargreaves	68 Farrow Street, Shaw, Oldham.	Cotton yarn salesman.

Oldham was not a town of remote mill owners, living in grand mansions, rather cotton mill directors had often worked their way up from humble origins and still lived in terraced houses. The most notable example

88 'Palmer Mills', *Oldham Chronicle*, Saturday, 22 August 1919, pg.11, col.2.

89 'New Capital Basis – Full Return of Spinning Company Changes – Turnovers and Reconstructions', *Oldham Chronicle, Textile Trade Supplement*, 31/12/1920; reprinted in *Cotton Spinning Companies Financial Review 1921* (Oldham: Oldham Chronicle, 1921).

90 Mule-equivalent reckons one ring spindle to be equivalent to 1·5 mule spindles.

of this was John Bunting who controlled twenty mills from his terraced house in Union Street.[91] The new directors of Palmer Mills were no exception; Hopwood, Bridge and Hargreaves all lived in small terraced houses (fig.51-53). However, Dixon's Struan House on Chamber Road was a larger detached house (fig.54).

By 24 December 1919, the date of the first return of share capital, all 30 000 shares had been issued to 34 persons. The distribution of shares was:

No. of Shares	No. of Persons
9700	1
9200	1
2500	1
2000	1
1000	1
500	4
300	1
200	9
100	15

The two largest shareholders were Harry Dixon and William Hopwood respectively, while William Bridge held only 1000 shares. The shareholders were geographically more widely dispersed than those of the old company:

Place	No.of Persons
Oldham	13
Stockport	7
Rochdale	4
Liverpool	2
Todmorden	2
Leigh	1
Huddersfield	1
Hebden Bridge	1
Bolton	1
Chelford, Cheshire	1
Blackpool	1

In contrast to the old company which was a 'democracy' of a large number of small shareholders, the new company was in the control of the group of the three investors from Oldham – Hopwood, Dixon and Bridge – who between them held 66% of the shares. No longer was it a Stockport company as it was now controlled from Oldham, only 20% of the shareholders coming from Stockport and these all held less than 500 shares each. Palmer Mills had been built in the 1880s as a challenge to the rise of the Oldham Limiteds, but had now succumbed to Oldham control.

But the premises behind the re-floating boom which had swept up Palmer Mill were wrong. The time of high profits did not last and the boom collapsed in 1921. William Hopwood's fall was as rapid as his rise. Although William Hopwood acted together with Harry Dixon and William Bridge, it was clear that he was the leading promoter. A native of Shaw born in 1862 he had started work in the Goats Mill of A. and A.Crompton and worked his way up from being a piecer, through self-actor minder and overlooker to become manager of Trent Mill, Shaw, subsequently becoming a director of this and several other companies. In 1914 he was involved with the purchase of Hare Mill, Todmorden, on behalf of a syndicate to rescue this ailing company which was renamed Mons Mill.[92] Subsequently in 1917 he was involved with the purchase of Thor Mill, Whitworth, which became Orama Mill. Although he denied starting the re-floating boom he was clearly one of the main promoters and during 1919 and 1920 he was involved in re-floating some thirty companies out of around 200. This left around 100 public spinning companies in

---

[91] D.A.Farnie, 'The Metropolis of Cotton Spinning, Machine Making and Mill Building' in Duncan Gurr and Julian Hunt, *The Cotton Mills of Oldham* (3rd edn, Oldham: Oldham Education and Leisure, 1998), 10.

[92] Roger N.Holden, 'The Troubled Origins and Demise of Mons Mill, Todmorden, 1907-1920', *Transactions of the Halifax Antiquarian Society*, 11 (2003), 138-56.

Lancashire which were not re-floated, although some of these underwent financial reconstruction and increased their capital. The boom centred on Oldham and the American branch of the cotton spinning trade.

The boom commenced in March 1919 but only became intense in August so Palmer was re-floated early and the promoters had already by that date begun looking outside Oldham. Other mills in Stockport re-floated were Vernon, Pear, Welkin Ring, Stockport Ring and Broadstone. Pear Mill was re-floated by the same three people as Palmer.[93] The usual method of operation, as at Palmer Mill, was to offer to buy the mill and the new company was floated in order to raise this purchase cost, the purchasers selling the mill to the new company for a considerable profit. They assumed that the exceptional profits of the last year were set to continue so that, even with the greatly increase capital, good dividends would be paid and the burden of loans could be serviced. Having collected considerable profits during this process Hopwood gave away large amounts to philanthropic causes, several churches in Shaw of all denominations from the Roman Catholics to the Salvation Army benefiting from this. This, together with the fact that he was already prominent in local politics, gained him a knighthood in the 1921 New Years Honours. 'Piecer to Knight - Sir William Hopwood of Shaw - A Notable Career' announced the headlines in the *Oldham Chronicle*, 'blunt, outspoken and shrewd, Sir William' it declared 'is a typical Lancashire man'.[94] By this time he had moved from his terraced house, but he still lived in Shaw at 'Sandycroft' on Rochdale Road.

The question might be asked as why the speculators went for an older mill like Palmer, much of whose machinery was admittedly obsolete and required replacement, although the blowing room machinery had recently been renewed. For comparison, all the machinery at Pear Mill was less than ten years old, dating from 1912, and the mules were longer than those at Palmer. The answer is simply that the speculators involved in reconstructing cotton mill companies seem to have taken no account of such factors, targeting old and new mills alike. Vernon Mill, which was next door to Palmer was of similar age, as were Anchor, Chadderton, Fern and Leesbrook Mills in Oldham.

Blunt and outspoken Hopwood may have been, shrewd he was not for by the end of that year he was in financial difficulties and was forced to resign his directorships, eventually going into bankruptcy with liabilities amounting to £244 351 6s 11d against which he had a single asset, a motor car valued at £50. During the bankruptcy proceedings William Hopwood attributed his failure to guaranteeing bank overdrafts for cotton mills and depreciation in the value of shares in these mills owing to the depression in trade.[95] He admitted that he kept no accounts, although claimed his secretary had done so, and comes over as having very little grasp of what was going on, being able to give little concrete detail as to his financial transactions. Maybe this was a studied forgetfulness but does not impress as somebody who had been both manager and director of cotton mills. When it was put to him that he thought that the exceptional post-war profits would last for a considerable time he blandly replied 'I thought so, everybody thought so'. Yet, as was pointed out, these exceptional profits had only arisen in the latter part of 1918 so this was hardly a reasonable assumption. Moreover, it was demonstrated that even if these profits had continued the re-floated companies could only have made dividends of around 5% rather than the 20% or more that Hopwood had claimed. Hopwood died in 1936. There was no suggestion that Hopwood and his fellow speculators were fraudulent in their activities but they clearly indulged in sharp practice. Their behaviour was reckless and evidently motivated by greed, offset by showings of philanthropy.

Harry Dixon and William Bridge survived for longer. Dixon took over as chairman at those companies where Hopwood had been chairman. He ran his companies as an informal grouping and maintained an office in Manchester for their administration. But he resigned from the board of Palmer on 28 April 1928 and by 1929 had forfeited his shares. He was declared bankrupt in 1931 with debts arising from unpaid share calls of £284 000. Younger than Hopwood being born in 1880, Dixon died in 1947. Less is known about William Bridge who resigned his directorship of Palmer Mills on 13 October 1928.[96]

The cotton industry had always been cyclical and people thought that it would recover again from the collapse of 1921 and indeed there was a slight recovery in 1925 and 1926. The *Oldham Chronicle* in its 'Textile Trades Review' for 1925 declared that it was the 'best time since the boom'. But this was a false

---

93 Roger N.Holden, 'Pear Mill, 1907-1929: A Stockport Cotton Spinning Company', *Manchester Region History Review*, 1:2 (1987), 23-9.

94 'Piecer to Knight', *Oldham Chronicle,* 1/1/1921, 11d.

95 'Mill Boom Profits-Sir W.Hopwood's Dealings with Sir John Leigh', *Oldham Chronicle,* 26/7/1924, 13.

96 Brian R.Law, *Oldham, Brave Oldham* (Oldham, 1999), 261-4. Farnie, 'Metropolis of Cotton Spinning', 10.

dawn and it took some years for the realisation that this time things were different as the First World War had disrupted the established trading patterns and the great export markets on which Lancashire depended had been lost. The American cotton spinning section of the trade, centred on Oldham and of which Palmer Mill was a part, was hardest hit, particularly by contraction of the Indian export market. This was also the section of the trade which had been most affected by the re-floating boom of 1919-20 which could now be seen to have been the height of folly as these mills now carried huge debt burdens which they could not re-pay. This likewise had a serious effect on the banks which had provided these loans in the first place resulting in Bank of England being instrumental in creating the Lancashire Cotton Corporation in 1929 with the object of buying up many of these mills and closing those considered to be obsolete and representing excess capacity. Individuals were also forced into bankruptcy as they held shares which were worthless and could not be sold.

The history of Palmer Mill through the 1920s before being sold to the Lancashire Cotton Corporation in 1930 was thus similar to many other companies in the industry. The company's bankers were Williams Deacon's, one of the Manchester banks who carried a considerable burden of the cotton industry's debt. No machinery replacement was carried out, and the mill continued to operate the same mules that had been installed when they were built. To survive the company continually called up share capital while paying no dividend in most years. The amount of share capital called up increased as follows:

1919	£45 000	£1 10s per share.
1924	£75 000	£2 10s per share.
1926	£90 000	£3 0s per share.
1928	£120 000	£4 0s per share.

The dividends declared between 1921 and 1929 inclusive were nil for all years except 1925 and 1926 when 5% dividends were declared.[97] The shareholders never saw the 25% returns promised in 1919.

The directorship of the company continued in a state of flux and by the 27 August 1929 had completely changed, consisting of:

Name	**Address**	**Occupation**
Frederick Alfred Tomlinson	'Bod Emryn', Tan-y-Bryn Road, Rhos-on-Sea, Colwyn Bay.	Cotton Broker.
Joseph Foster	'Holloway', Park Crescent, Southport.	Director of companies.
Ernest Hirst	'Wood Cottage', Todmorden.	Director of companies.
Edward Charles Woolmer	'Parkfield', Trafalgar Road, Birkdale, Southport.	Director of companies.

The directorship was now more geographically dispersed than before and consisted mainly of people who were professional company directors; it is possible that these were people who had been put in by the Bank. The company's bank overdraft stood at £146 272 0s 3d. The loan account stood at £34 776 8s 2d. At this date 13 750 shares, out of 30 000 had been forfeited through failure to pay calls on shares, the biggest defaulter being Harry Dixon with 12 100 shares; he had evidently increase his initial holding of 9 700 shares. A scheme of arrangement with the company's creditors was sanctioned by Chancery Court hearing on 13 March 1930 and this cleared the way for the sale of the mill to the Lancashire Cotton Corporation.[98] As a result the winding up of the company was sanctioned on the 2 May 1930, although the final winding up meeting was not held until 19 October 1938. Palmer Mill was sold to the Lancashire Cotton Corporation for a total of £214 419 16s 4d, £3230 13s 4d in cash, the rest in stocks and shares.[99] This, it will be noted, is £100 000 less than the mill changed hands for in 1919.

---

97 'Spinners' Dividends for Five Years', *Oldham Chronicle*, 2/1/1926, pg.11. *Oldham Chronicle* Textile Trades Review (annual, published on last Saturday of old year or first Saturday of new year). A figure of 27% is actually given for Palmer Mills dividend in 1925 but a note in the 'Textile Trades Review' states that this 'includes bonus calls'. The actual announcement of dividends gives 5%; 'Stocktakings' *Oldham Chronicle* 21/3/1925, 13b; 19/9/1925, 14d.

98 'Palmer Mills-A Scheme of Arrangement Sanctioned', *Oldham Chronicle,* 15/3/1930, 14e.

99 Details of winding-up and price paid by the Lancashire Cotton Corporation are in TNA BT31/32315/158825. The length of time which elapsed before the final winding-up is not unusual.

The Lancashire Cotton Corporation did not operate the mill for very long. Even in 1919 some of the machinery had been considered to be obsolete while the rather complex and congested nature of the site would have compared unfavourably with mills built just before the First World War. Thus, with excess capacity in the industry, it would have been a mill not worth keeping. The No.1 Mill had in fact ceased operating in March 1930, before the Lancashire Cotton Corporation take over, but it was restarted later that year, on Monday 6 October, and the intention was to operate the whole of No.2 Mill, only three-quarters of which was then running.[100] This coincided with the re-opening by the Lancashire Cotton Corporation of the adjoining Vernon No.1 Mill, which had been stopped since August 1927. This was said to be because of steadily increasing demands for their standard yarns. However, this revival was short lived as three months later, in January 1931, Palmer Mills were closed completely, and it would appear that they never operated again, although they continued to be listed in Worrall's *Lancashire Textile Directory* until 1933.[101] The Lancashire Cotton Corporation had acquired five mills in Stockport in addition to Palmer; these were Welkin, Vernon, India, Travis Brook and Kingston. By June 1932 only Welkin and Kingston were operating and all the others were subsequently disposed of. Welkin was a ring spinning mill, originally known as Ark, dating from around 1908 while Kingston was a much older mill that had been totally re-equipped for ring spinning. By 1959 only Welkin Mill still operated and this ceased soon after.

---

100 'Cotton Cloud's Silver Lining-Two Stockport Mills to Re-open' *Stockport Advertiser,* 3/10/1930, 11d-e. 'Stockport Mills Re-open - Vernon and Palmer No.1', *Stockport Advertiser,* 10/10/1930, 11e-f.

101 'Stockport's Cotton Gloom', *Stockport Advertiser,* 24/6/1932, 8e, reports that Palmer Mills have been closed for 18 months.

Fig.55 Palmer No.2 Mill from the south. Meadow Mill is visible in the background. (15/09/1996)

Fig.56 Palmer No.2 Mill (left) and Vernon No.1 Mill (right) viewed from the south-east. (06/12/1998)

LANCASTER STREET
N
MERSEY STREET
QUEEN STREET
ST.MARY'S WAY
No.2 Mill
Engine House
0
100ft
0
50m
Approx. scales only.
RIVER GOYT
PALMER MILLS, STOCKPORT
BLOCK PLAN - 1989

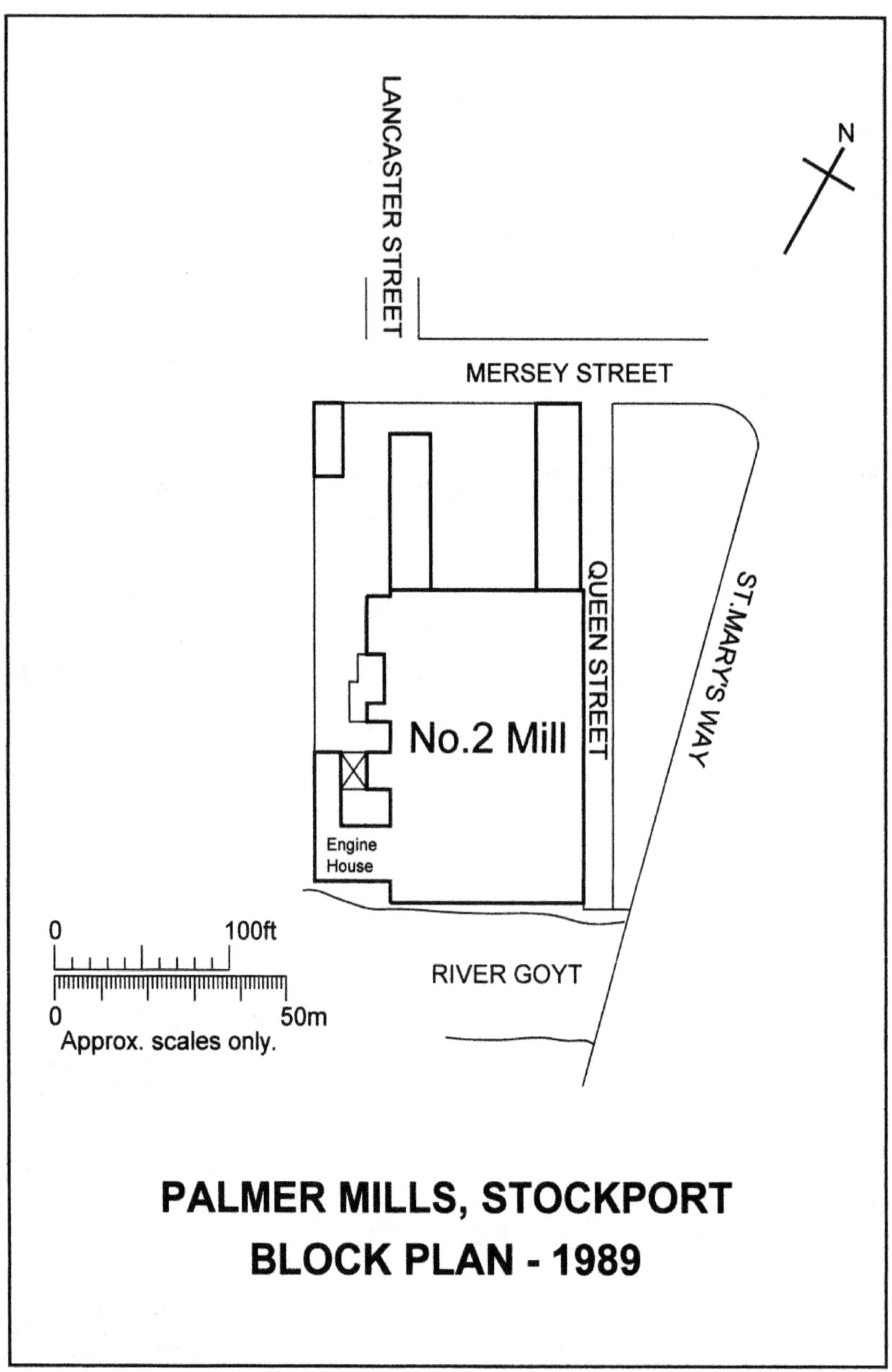

Fig.57

12. FROM 1933 TO 1999

The mills must have remained empty and unused until 1937 when they were purchased by Kayley Ltd. for unknown purposes. They immediately sold on the western part of the site for an extension to the gas works, although in the event nothing seems to have been built on this area (fig.1). This included the No.1 Mill, the boiler house and Mersey House which were all demolished. The walling where the two mills were joined was repaired. During the Second World War the remaining buildings were requisitioned by the War Department for the manufacture of Royal Air Force uniforms. In around 1940 a number of alterations were carried out. The Old Mill and the single storey section between it and No.2 Mill were cleared. Two single storey office wings were constructed on either side of this area (fig.1, 38 & 57) and large wagon door openings inserted at ground floor level facing Mersey Street where it had originally connected to the Old Mill (fig.39). A passenger lift was installed adjoining the staircase. It is not clear when the mill was returned to civilian use or again to what uses it was put but a further passenger lift was installed in 1953-1954; this is probably the plain brick tower which was attached to the west side of the mill between the stair tower and the yarn hoist (fig.36 & 44). Subsequently the mill was in multiple occupation by a variety of businesses, while remaining in the ownership of Kayley Ltd.[102]

During 1995 English Heritage carried out an exercise to review the representation of textile mills in the list of buildings considered to be of architectural or historic interest.[103] Buildings on this list are subject to restrictions on demolition or change which would significantly alter their character. Some mills were already included but it was recommended that further mills be added in order to preserve a representative collection of mills. This exercise involved a consultation beforehand in which the proposed list was presented to owners of buildings affected and for public discussion. Palmer Mill was included in this preliminary listing but was not included in the final list, released on the 5 November 1996. The reason given for not listing was that the owner had demonstrated that the present building represented the surviving part of a once more substantial complex, English Heritage stating that 'In instances where a mill complex had undergone alteration or part demolition, the presumption was against listing, unless there was compelling evidence that the incomplete site was of outstanding significance'. While as we have demonstrated the mill was indeed the surviving fragment of a larger complex, it is somewhat disappointing that English Heritage allowed themselves to be swayed by this argument, as Palmer No.2 Mill was a complete structure in its own right, was largely as built and was the most complete example of the construction illustrated in the drawings accompanying Stott & Sons 1885 patent. Moreover other mills were included in the list even though only surviving parts of a larger complex. Vernon Mill, immediately next door to Palmer Mill, is an example of this as it is also the survivor of two mills and has undergone considerable alteration, particularly after fire damage in 1902 (fig.10 & 11).[104]

The reason for the owner's opposition to listing soon became clear when at the end of 1998 proposals were announced for the demolition of the mill and construction of a retail unit on its site. So Councillor Burtinshaw's fears that the site would be used for shops was coming to pass 114 years later. Demolition commenced late in May 1999, the site being cleared by mid-August (fig.58-68). Subsequently a retail unit was built on the site but some of the cast-iron and steel work from the mill was recovered during demolition and used to create a sculpture in memory of the mill (fig.69-73). This has a plaque which proclaims, unfortunately with an incorrect date for the construction of the mill:

> This Art Feature has been erected with material salvaged from PALMER MILL, which stood on this site between 1893 and 1999. The design intends to reflect the Magnificence of the Mill and the Industrial Heritage of Stockport. Liz Kayley. Designer and Artist. 30.3.2000.

---

[102] Information in this paragraph from John Rose Associates, *Palmer Mill, Portwood, Stockport: Archaeological Report* (Poynton: John Rose Associates, 1999), 3. This actually refers to single storey weaving sheds being demolished, this must refer to the single storey section between No.2 and the Old Mill.

[103] English Heritage, *Manchester Mills: Understanding Listing* (London: English Heritage, 1995).

[104] 'Heritage bid to save dark satanic mills', *Manchester Metro News*, 16/6/1995. 'Thirty Historic Manchester Mills Are Listed' Department of the National Heritage News Release DNH338/96, 5/11/1996. Dr.Martin Cherry, Head of Listing, English Heritage, pers.comm. to the author 23/1/1997.

The other part of the mill to survive is the basement wall along the river bank which no doubt provided a convenient retaining wall for levelling of the site (fig.68 & 70). The retail unit itself has arched windows designed to reflect those of the mill, particularly those in the engine house. (fig.69, 70 & 74)

In the 1960s Nikolaus Pevsner found the views over Stockport from the north to be 'grim but splendid'. But his revisers in the 2000s dropped this comment; presumably they found that the views were now neither grim nor splendid. The demolition of Palmer Mill contributed to the loss of this grim splendour, which has been replaced by the twenty-first century common-places of motorway, car park, shopping centre and super-store (fig.75-77).[105]

[105] Nikolaus Pevsner, *The Buildings of England: South Lancashire* (Harmondsworth: Penguin Books, 1969), 121. Clare Hartwell, Matthew Hyde and Nikolaus Pevsner, *The Buildings of England: Lancashire: Manchester and the South-East* (New Haven & London: Yale University Press, 2004), 233.

Fig.58 No.2 Mill from the north-west just after demolition had commenced with floor boards stacked ready for removal on the top floor window sills. (25/5/1999)

Fig.59 Detail of the top floor windows on the north wall of No.2 Mill just after demolition had commenced with floor boards stacked ready for removal on the top floor window sills. Also visible are the brick arches running parallel to the wall and terminating with a half-arch adjoining the wall. (25/5/1999)

Fig.60 View taken during demolition of No.2 Mill showing the construction of the mill. To the rear is the original yarn hoist. (4/7/1999)

Fig.61 The east wall of No.2 Mill during demolition. At the top of the part demolished section of the wall can be seen the secondary beams still attached to the cross beam which was originally supported by the brick wall. (15/6/1999)

Fig.62 Demolition of the north wall of No.2 Mill in progress. (12/6/1999)

Fig.63 Demolition of the north wall of No.2 Mill in progress, showing one of the cast-iron columns embedded in the wall. (12/6/1999)

Fig.64 Staircase and water tower of No.2 Mill viewed from the south-east during demolition. This view shows the lift tower on the south side that was added after 1937. (9/7/1999)

Fig.65 Main girder removed during demolition of No.2 Mill. (14/06/1999)

Fig.66 Secondary girder removed during demolition, complete with brackets for attaching to main girders. (14/06/1999)

Fig.67 Demolition of No.2 Mill; only the water and staircase tower left standing. To the left can be seen the chimney of Pear Mill and the engine house of Vernon No.1 Mill. (23/7/1999)

Fig.68 No.2 Mill reduced to a pile of rubble, but the basement wall on the south, next to the river, was left to form a retaining wall for the development of the site. In the background can be seen the twin towers and chimney of Meadow Mill. (23/7/1999)

Fig.69 A year after demolition of No.2 Mill the new retail unit on the site is almost complete with some of the iron and steel work of the mill re-erected as a sculpture. (11/6/2000)

Fig.70 The new retail unit with the basement wall of No.2 Mill formed into a retaining wall. (11/06/2000)

Fig.71 (left) The memorial sculpture formed by iron and steel work from the No.2 Mill. (24/02/2017)
Fig.72 (right) Detail of the memorial sculpture, which correctly shows the bolting of the main girders to the column head. (24/02/2017)

Fig.73 Although rather faint and upside down, the Leeds Steel Works stamp can be seen on one of the main girders incorporated into the memorial sculpture. (24/02/2017)

Fig.74 Originally Courts, the retail unit later became a Dunelm Mill outlet. This is taken from the same place as fig.38. (24/02/2017)

Fig.75 Portwood in the 1960s, part of Nikolaus Pevsner's 'grim but splendid' view over Stockport. Palmer No.2 Mill can be seen to the left of the cooling tower and the waterless gas holder. To its left is Vernon No.1 Mill, behind which is Pear Mill. Much of the foreground is occupied by the Park Mills with Faulder's Cocoa Works, originally Park Bridge Mill, in the centre of the view.

Stockport Local Heritage Library.

Fig.76 View over Portwood from Tiviot Dale in the early 1980s. The motorway was opened in 1982 and on the right Park Mills have been demolished, but Faulder's Cocoa Works still stands. Palmer No.2 Mill is visible in the centre of the view, to the left of the gas holders. To the left of Palmer is Vernon No.1 Mill, still with chimney. Beyond Vernon can be seen the chimney and water tower of Pear Mill. (01/1983)

Fig.77 Over thirty years later, the motorway is partly masked by trees. Palmer No.2 Mill has long gone, the roofs of the Peel Centre can be seen, but Vernon No.1 and Pear Mills still stand. (26/12/2016)

DOCUMENTARY SOURCES

The National Archives (TNA), Kew.

BT31 Board of Trade; Companies Registration Office; Files of Dissolved Companies:

BT31/14779/20252 Palmer Mills Co.Ltd, 1885.

BT31/32315/158825 Palmer Mills (1919) Ltd, 1919.

BT31/14670/14934 Vernon Cotton Spinning Co.Ltd, 1881.

Lancashire Archives, Preston.

DDPSL Platt-Saco-Lowell Archive.

DDPSL/3 Howard & Bullough Ltd.

DDPSL/3/8 Weekly Totals and Value of Machinery Ordered.

DDPSL/3/8/3 Jul.1905-Dec.1907, 1, 12.

DDPSL/3/8/4 Jan.1908-Feb.1911, 36, 39, 153.

DDPSL/3/8/5 Feb.1911-Feb.1914, 8, 11, 20, 22, 31, 42 ,87, 90, 116.

DDPSL/4 Asa Lees & Co.Ltd.

DDPSL/4/3/1 Carding Engine Order Book 1884-1889, pg.51, Order E657, Palmer Mills Co.Ltd., Stockport, 27 July 1886; 187, Order E789, Palmer Mills Co.Ltd., Stockport, 3 May 1889.

DDPSL/4/4/4 Slubbing, Intermediate and Roving Frames Order Book 1885-1888, 43-45, Orders R879, R880 & R881, Palmer Mills Co.Ltd., Stockport, 27 July 1886.

DDPSL/4/4/5 Slubbing, Intermediate and Roving Frames Order Book 1888-1889, 156-158, Orders R1192-R1194, Palmer Mills Co.Ltd., Stockport, 3 May 1889.

DDPSL/4/22/4 Tin Work for Mules & Twiners Book 1885-1887, 63-64 Orders M753 & M754, Palmer Mills Co.Ltd., Stockport, 27 July 1886. [NB. The Mule Order Book for this date does not survive.]

DDPSL/4/22/6 Tin Work for Mules & Twiners Book 1889-1891, 1-2 Orders M1099 & M1100, Palmer Mills Co.Ltd., Stockport, 3 May 1889. [NB. The Mule Order Book for this date does not survive.]

Stockport Metropolitan Borough Council, Planning Dept., Building Regulation Plans for Stockport, No.1235, Palmer Mills Co.Ltd, 4 September 1885, consisting of:

Ground Plan (Stott & Sons drawing no.6172) 9/6/1885,

Block Plan (Stott & Sons drawing no.6243) 3/7/1885,

Transverse Section (Stott & Sons drawing no.6212) 27/6/1885,

Roving Shed Privies (Stott & Sons drawing no.6601) 3/9/1885.

These plans were inspected on 11/5/1989 but are believed to subsequently have been destroyed. No plans for the No.2 Mill could be located.

Ordnance Survey Maps.

1848 1:10 560 Lancashire sheet 112.

1851 1:1056 Stockport sheet 6.

1872 1:2500 Cheshire sheet 10.15.

1892 1:2500 Cheshire sheet 10.15.

1895 1:1056 Stockport sheet 6.

1907 1:2500 Cheshire sheet 10.15.

1934 1:2500 Cheshire sheet 10.15.

1960 1:2500 National grid sheet SJ9090.

1997 1:1250 National Grid sheet SJ9090NW (digital update).

Directories.

Wardle & Bentham, *The Commercial Directory 1814-15*.

Wardle & Pratt, *The Commercial Directory 1816-17*.

Pigot & Dean, *New Directory of Manchester and Salford 1821-22*.

Edward Baines, *History, Directory and Gazetteer of the County Palatine of Lancaster 1824*.

Pigot, *National Commercial Directory for Cheshire 1828-8*.

Williams, *Commercial Directory of Stockport, Preston, Wigan &c. 1845*.

Bagshaw, *History, Gazetteer and Directory of the County Palatine of Chester 1850*.

Slater, *Directory of Manufacturing Districts Round Manchester 1851.*
White, *History, Gazetteer and Directory of Cheshire 1860.*
Morris, *Commercial Directory and Gazetteer of Cheshire 1864.*
Worrall, *Directory of Stockport 1872.*
Kelly, *Directory of Cheshire 1878.*

Worrall's *Lancashire Textile Directory* published 1884-1930 under the title *The Cotton Spinners' and Manufacturers Directory for Lancashire* and from 1931-1970 under the title *The Lancashire Textile Industry.*

Skinner's *Cotton Trade Directory of the World*, published annually from 1923.

Press (detailed references in footnotes)
Oldham Chronicle.
Stockport Advertiser.
Textile Manufacturer.
Textile Recorder.

SELECT BIBLIOGRAPHY

Peter Arrowsmith, *Stockport: A History* (Stockport: Stockport Metropolitan Borough Council, 1997).

Owen Ashmore (Ed), *The Industrial Archaeology of Stockport* (Manchester: Dept.of Extra-Mural Studies, University of Manchester, 1975).

Douglas A.Farnie and David J.Jeremy (eds), *The Fibre that Changed the World: The Cotton Industry in International Perspective, 1600-1990s* (Oxford: Oxford University Press, 2004).

Roger N.Holden, *Stott & Sons: Architects of the Lancashire Cotton Mill* (Lancaster: Carnegie 1998).

Roger N.Holden, 'Water Supplies for Steam-powered Textile Mills', *Industrial Archaeology Review*, 21:1 (1999), 41-51.

John Jewkes and E.M.Grey, *Wages and Labour in the Lancashire Cotton Spinning Industry* (Manchester: Manchester University Press, 1935).

Mike Williams with Douglas A.Farnie, *Cotton Mills in Greater Manchester* (Preston: Carnegie, 1992).

APPENDIX
OCCUPATIONS OF SHAREHOLDERS, 1885

From the Summary of Capital and Shares. 23 January 1885. This lists alphabetically the occupations found in the shareholders list and the number of shareholders with that occupation.

Occupation	No. of Persons	Occupation	No. of Persons
Accountant	2	Lady	1
Agent	3	Leather Merchant	1
Architect	3	Letter Carrier	1
Assistant Overseer	1	M.D. [*sic*]	1
At home	1	Machine Brick Manufacturer	1
At school	3	Manufacturer	1
Bleach Works Manager	1	Married Woman	5
Bleacher	1	Mechanic	1
Boiler Maker	1	Mechanical Engineer	1
Bookkeeper	1	Mill Manager	2
Bookseller	1	Mineral Water Manufacturer	1
Brass Founder	2	Minor	1
Brewer	1	Musician	1
Butcher	5	Newsagent	2
Calico Printer	1	Newspaper Proprietor	2
Candlewick Spinner	1	Not Stated	12
Card Nailer	1	Nut & Bolt Forger	1
Carder	2	Organisation[106]	4
Carrier	3	Out of Business	1
Cashier	1	Overlooker	1
Cheese Factor	1	Overseers Clerk	1
Chemical Works Manager	1	Pattern Maker	1
Clerk	2	Pie Maker	1
Coal Dealer	1	Piecer	1
Coal Merchant	1	Pipelayer	1
Company Secretary	1	Pork Butcher	4
Contractor	1	Post Office [*sic*]	1
Corn Agent	1	Printer & Stationer	1
Corn Merchant	1	Provision Dealer	7
Cotton Broker	1	Provision Dealer & Beerseller	1
Cotton Carder	1	Provision Merchant	1
Cotton Doubler	1	Publican	1
Cotton Machinist	1	Railway Inspector	1
Cotton Mill Manager	1	Registrar of Births & Deaths	1
Cotton Operative	1	Roller Coverer	1
Cotton Spinner	2	Salesman	2
Draper	4	School Teacher	1
Earthenware Manufacturer	2	Science Teacher	1
Engine Driver	1	Seedsman	1
Engineer	2	Self-Actor Minder	6
Estate Agent	1	Servant	1
Farmer	1	Shipowner	1
Gardener	1	Shipper	1
General Dealer	2	Skip Manufacturer	1
General Draper	1	Solicitor	1
Gentleman	1	Spindle & Fly Maker	1
Greengrocer	1	Spinner	1
Grocer	3	Spinster	4
Grover & Corn Dealer	1	Stamp Office [*sic*]	1
Grocer & Provision Dealer	1	Stationer	1

[106] One Trades Union, two Friendly Societies, one Co-Operative Society.

Occupation	No. of Persons	Occupation	No. of Persons
Hat Manufacturer	2	Surgeon	3
Hatter	4	Surgeons Assistant	1
Hatters	1	Tailor	2
Hatters Machinist	1	Tin Plate Worker	2
Herbalist	1	Tobacconist	2
Housekeeper	3	[Unclear]	1
Housemaid	1	Vicar	1
Innkeeper	2	Violinist	1
Insurance Accountant	1	Widow	1
		Total	194

Fig.78 Endpiece. Aerial view of Palmer No.2 Mill from the south-east. The white building facing the mill across Mersey Street is the Coach and Horses Public House. The engine house of Vernon No.1 Mill can be seen bottom right. Vernon No.2 Mill occupied the area between here and Queen Street running along the right side of Palmer No.2 Mill (fig.4). (10/05/1989)

© Crown Copyright. Historic England Archive

Front cover: Palmer No.2 Mill. North-west corner and water tower. (6/12/1998)

Rear cover: Palmer No.2 Mill in the snow. In the background the long façade of Meadow Mill. On the skyline, Broadstone and Houldsworths Mills at Reddish. (28/1/1996)

www.ingramcontent.com/pod-product-compliance
Lightning Source LLC
LaVergne TN
LVHW081150110826
845149LV00008B/1614

* 9 7 8 0 9 9 5 6 9 7 7 1 3 *